Trade Unions:
the Logic of Collective Action

Colin Crouch was born in 1944 and educated at
the London School of Economics and Political
Science and at Nuffield College, Oxford. He is now
a reader in sociology at the LSE. He is the
author of *The Student Revolt* (1970), *Class Conflict
and the Industrial Relations Crisis* (1977), *The Politics
of Industrial Relations* (Fontana, 1979; revised edition
forthcoming) and of articles and Fabian Society
pamphlets in the fields of social stratification,
industrial relations and social policy; and editor of
Stress and Contradiction in Modern Capitalism (1975:
with L. N. Lindberg and others), *British Political
Sociology Yearbook*, Volume III: *Participation in
Politics* (1977), *The Resurgence of Class Conflict in
Western Europe since 1968*, two volumes (1978: with
A. Pizzorno) and *State and Economy in Contemporary
Capitalism* (1979). He is a former chairman of the
Fabian Society.

Fontana New Sociology

Editor: Gavin Mackenzie, lecturer in sociology at the
University of Cambridge and fellow of Jesus College,
Cambridge

Trade Unions:
the Logic of Collective Action

Colin Crouch

Fontana Paperbacks

First published by Fontana Paperbacks 1982
Copyright © Colin Crouch 1982
Set in 10/12 pt Lasercomp Plantin
Made and printed in Great Britain by
William Collins Sons & Co. Ltd, Glasgow

for **Joan, Daniel
and Benjamin**

Contents

Editor's Preface

This series is designed to provide comprehensive and authoritative analyses of issues at the centre of contemporary sociological discussion. Each volume will therefore present and evaluate both the major theoretical standpoints and the empirical findings relevant to specific problems within sociology; but, in addition, each volume will itself be an original contribution to our understanding of that topic. So the series will be of value to laymen and professional sociologists alike.

The focus will be on contemporary Britain, although comparison with the institutional orders of other advanced societies and, indeed, with pre-capitalist social formations, will form an integral part of each book. Analyses of the division of labour, its structure and consequences, of social class and other forms of inequality, and of the institutions and the distribution of power in politics and in industry, will dominate the collection. Yet this emphasis will not preclude discussion of other aspects of contemporary British society, such as the family, urbanism or lawbreaking.

The series is based on three premises. First, the primary concern of sociology as an academic discipline is the analysis of *social structure* – of the institutions and social processes characteristic of advanced industrial societies. Second, the distinction between 'sociological theory' and 'empirical sociology', found so often within the subject, is false. Finally, sociological explanation incorporates historical explanation; and 'social' institutions cannot be examined in isolation from 'economic' or 'political' ones. Indeed, one of the most important changes now taking place in the social sciences is the recognition that the boundaries which hitherto have separated one discipline from another are artificial. On these premises, the series determines to help us understand the functioning of the society in which we live.

Gavin Mackenzie
Jesus College, Cambridge

Author's Preface

My aim in this book is to set out a rationality of trade unionism. This phrase has two different meanings, corresponding to the two audiences for whom the book has been written. First, it is directed at general readers interested in understanding trade unions. Understanding the behaviour of modern British trade unions is often regarded as a difficult task, their being commonly regarded as irrational, tradition-bound or plain bloody-minded. But many of the apparent mysteries of union behaviour can be made explicable if one examines the context in which they operate, the opportunities and limitations confronting them. This is what I have tried to do.

To make something explicable does not necessarily mean to justify it; this book is not a *defence* of trade unions, but an analysis. It should, however, be a book that is relevant to political debate, providing raw material for both justifications and criticisms of trade-union action. It is a rather abstract book; I have not retraced a particular historical record or related detailed case histories, though I have made use of several real-life examples.

The second intended readership comprises students of sociology and other social sciences. For them, too, I want to make union behaviour explicable; but I am also concerned that they give some consideration to the methodological question: what does it *mean* to make something explicable? In this academic sense my aims are rather more polemical. Generalizing a little extravagantly, it can be said that there are three ways of explaining social behaviour.

First, one may set out the broad outlines of the structures of the society within which the behaviour takes place, and account for it by showing how it suits the logic of those structures. This is usually, but not exclusively, the hall-mark of traditional Marxist accounts (e.g., trade unions are compelled to act the way they do because the society in which they exist is a capitalist one). Second, behaviour may be explained by showing that the manifest or latent values and beliefs of the actors predisposed them to act the way they did. This is very widespread among contemporary sociologists of all kinds, particularly because of the importance of surveys of opinion as a distinctive sociological research method. Among the social sciences sociologists are generally regarded as the experts of opinions and attitudes, and it is for accounts of these that people usually turn to them. Finally, however, behaviour can be seen as the outcome of rational choices by actors who have calculated how best to maximize their interests given the constraints of their situation. Elements of this approach can be found in all social sciences, but its heartland is economics.

I do not see any necessary contradiction between these three approaches to explanation; rather they are mutually indispensable. Starting from the assumption of calculative rational choice, one can easily build into one's account of the constraints of the situation those wider structural forces in which Marxists are interested; and one's account of the choice process can and should include reference to the beliefs and values which determine people's evaluations of desired ends and means. This is what I have tried to do in these pages.

However, there is a tendency within current sociology to downgrade the third, rational choice, approach, in favour of the other two. Although Marx himself often used a rational calculus to account for social action, contemporary Marxists have been particularly responsible for this. In the past few decades they have spent much time adding accounts of values (or ideology) to their structural starting point, but the effect has often been to rule out any consideration of human action as involving choice. The existing tendency for sociology to be concerned primarily with attitudes combines with the Marxist stress on ideology to rule out consideration of social actors as rational beings, consciously selecting their courses of action from a limited and usually structured set of alternatives.

This book therefore swims against the current tide of sociological fashion, especially in this field of industrial relations where Marxist writers have recently come to dominate; though, to switch metaphors, I can point to a number of other 'straws in the wind' moving in the opposite direction from that tide: Abercrombie, Hill and Turner's (1980) criticism of reliance on assumptions of a 'dominant ideology' in Marxist explanations of the behaviour of subordinate classes; Parkin's (1979) general critique of recent Marxist sociology, and Heath's (1976) assertion of the place of rational choice in social explanation.

What emerges from all this is the beginnings of a *theory* of trade unionism. This book cannot claim to constitute such a theory; it is directed at an elementary, introductory level and deals with only a number of all the relevant variables. But it is intended to provide the basis of such a theory.

The text needs two final points of clarification. First, I have not spent time thrashing out a definition of trade unions, but have assumed a common-sense approach: a trade union is an organization of employees who have combined together to improve their returns from and conditions at work. This leaves two important complications: (i) the possibility of a distinction between the members of the union and the organization itself and (ii) the tendency for unions to become involved in political issues going beyond a strict definition of work-related issues. These complications are the subject of the two final chapters.

Second, some readers may be annoyed at the oversimplifications of issues and situations which they will find here, and will want to add a mass of ifs and buts and qualifications to the argument as soon as it gets started. I ask them to accept with patience the maxim that theory can only start with simple cases. If too many variables are admitted at an early stage, arguments become so complex that they say nothing at all. In the social sciences we are rarely able to set up laboratory conditions and examine pure cases under controlled variables. We can, however, set up our arguments this way, examining complex situations piece by piece, gradually building up the number of variables as we come to understand the simpler, basic ones.

Gavin Mackenzie has been a model editor, exercising great patience with a succession of inadequate and tardy drafts, and offering considerable help with the content even on the several points where he disagrees with me. Since, despite this, I did not take all his advice, he cannot be blamed for the result.

I am grateful to the editors of *Sociologie du Travail* for permission to use, as the base for chapters 5 and 6, parts of my article 'La politique dans les relations industrielles: gouvernements et revendications syndicales dans less années 1970', published in no. 4/79 of that journal.

1 Approaches to the Study of Trade Unions

Whereas only nuclear physicists study the process of nuclear fission, and sociologists have a monopoly of the study of social mobility, no one discipline can claim research on trade unionism as its own. It is one of those subjects which is defined by the world at large, not by an academic discipline, so scholars from many different specialisms are entitled to use their expertise on it. Political scientists sometimes examine the internal processes of trade unions as examples of small polities. Economists are interested in the economic consequences of unions' action and in interpreting their behaviour in economic terms. And, most important of all, there is in the United Kingdom and the United States of America a large body of industrial-relations specialists who are defined, not by any academic discipline – they come from several – but by their subject of interest.

Which of these different approaches should be included in an assessment of the *sociology* of the subject? Since one's interest is mainly in what is known rather than who knows it, one's prejudice should be in favour of inclusion and one should not quibble too much about subject boundaries. Economists present some difficulties, since they work very much within their own tight and elaborate theoretical framework, though some of the greatest labour economists, such as E. H. Phelps Brown and John Dunlop, have cast their net far wider and have adapted the perspectives of other subjects. But there is a case for sociologists treating the work of political scientists and industrial-relations spe-

cialists as variants of their own subject where trade-union
studies are concerned. The boundary between sociology
and political science is never very clear, only being sharply
distinct when the latter insists on limiting its focus to
formally political and governmental institutions with no
reference to the wider social context. Political scientists
studying trade unions have automatically strayed from that
path and can indeed have a very easy dialogue with sociologists.

The industrial-relations school, containing individuals
from heterogeneous backgrounds, does include some
straightforward sociologists within its ranks, especially
among younger researchers. Earlier generations had more
diverse origins: historians, lawyers, politics specialists,
economists. As such they came from no particular theoretical schools, and found their unity and mode of dis-
course in the substance of their object of study rather than
in their academic perspectives. This has imposed a distinctive character on British industrial-relations research,
which is mainly descriptive and factual and – an important
point – closely associated with practice, with advising employers, trade unions and governments.

Insofar as this school has a theory, it is that of the
industrial-relations system as a network of rules developed
by the late Alan Flanders (1970: esp. p. 86; see also Clegg,
1979: ch. 1). Although his work was highly original, he
drew much from the theoretical approach of the American
John Dunlop (1958), whose concept of an industrial-relations system was strongly influenced by the social theories
of the late Talcott Parsons – who was a sociologist, the
dominant American sociologist of this century. I therefore
have little hesitation in including the work of the industrial-
relations school under the heading of sociology. The es-
sence of sociology is the explanation of human conduct in
terms of the laws governing the behaviour of collectivities,
groups (formal and informal) and organizations. In other
words, human behaviour is not treated as simply the product of the wills of a mass of individual psyches; neither is

it regarded as totally random and unpredictable. In this sense the industrial-relations school, with its stress on institutional regularities, is a sociological school. Henceforth I shall therefore include the works of both political scientists and industrial-relations specialists simply as contributions to the sociology of trade unionism.

Taken thus extensively, the sociology of trade unionism encompasses a large literature. While there remain great gaps in our knowledge, we know more about trade unions than we do of many other institutions in our society. This is partly because industrial relations are among the few areas of social enquiry, research into which attracts the interest of governments and employers. But it is also because, for a variety of reasons, many sociologists are interested in studying trade unions. There are also several good introductory books for students and general readers which scan the field of existing knowledge and distil its most important findings.[1] In this book I shall not try to add yet another contribution to this list, but shall develop one particular approach to the subject. However, in a book that is intended to be introductory it is important to give readers some idea of the scope of the field. In the remainder of this chapter I shall attempt a brief survey of this kind, and then outline my approach.

Given the large and varied literature on trade unions, it is not possible to do justice to all the differences among schools and the disagreements over interpretation. However, at the risk of leaving some people out and putting others with uncongenial company, it is reasonable to offer the threefold classification of institutional pluralists, radicals and Marxists. Those familiar with the literature will see a little similarity here with Alan Fox's (1973 and 1974a and b) classification of unitary, pluralist and radical frameworks of analysis of industrial relations – minus the unitarists but plus the Marxists, some of whom have already shown that they cannot be included as mere radicals by offering a 'radical critique' of Fox's 'radical critique' (e.g., Wood and Elliott, 1977).

By unitarists Fox meant that school which stresses the extent of shared interests between employers and workers, and which therefore tends to regard conflict as rather unnecessary, the result of misunderstanding or mischief; in other words, as pathological. This is no minor current of opinion within the society at large; indeed, Fox treats it as probably the dominant one. It describes the prevailing view of large numbers of employers, and probably of many workers as well. It has also loomed large in industrial sociology, particularly in the USA – most explicitly in the work of Elton Mayo, to which I shall give some attention later. Why, then, do I not include unitarists in my classification of contemporary British approaches to the study of trade unions? Rather significantly, perhaps, many of the industrial sociologists who have adopted this approach have had little to say about trade unions as such; they tend to stray to the psychological borders of the discipline, explaining workers' behaviour in terms of problems of individual psychology. This was outstandingly true of Mayo who, it has often been remarked, made virtually no references at all to unions in his voluminous output of writings on industrial workers. Nevertheless, there are proponents of what might be called a unitary approach among the major figures of British industrial-relations research – for example, B. C. Roberts (1968: 9–34; 1971) and D. F. MacDonald (1976). But it is striking that, among the students of trade unionism, these remain isolated voices, hardly constituting schools. This is extraordinary when one considers that their approach is that favoured by large numbers of non-academic practitioners of industrial relations, especially on the managerial side. Whether the explanation for this lies in the intrinsic 'faultiness' of the unitary perspective or in the incorrigible radicalism of most sociologists specializing in trade unionism is an interesting question and one on which subsequent chapters will contribute some observations – on both sides. However, for immediate purposes it is enough to draw attention to the small size within British trade-union research of any school dealing mainly in terms of a unity of interests between employers and employees. All three dominant schools take conflict more or less for granted, though they mean very different things by conflict.

Institutional pluralists

In the absence of much of a unitary school, the institutional pluralists occupy the position of the subject's Establishment. The central concern of this approach is to describe the institutions of industrial relations accurately and in particular to insist on the centrality of collective bargaining to trade-union activity and to the conduct of industrial relations. They have emphasized how union practices emerge, not from any centrally imposed pattern, but from the actions of workers and managers on the shop floor coming to terms with each other – in the words of the title of a recent article, 'The inevitable growth of informality' (Terry, 1977; see also Clegg, 1979: 232 ff). Trade-union organizations are seen as having the difficult task of accommodating these emergent practices and domesticating them so that they may be located in a framework of rules.

That there will be conflicts of interest between employers and workers is taken for granted, and the conflicts involved are approached in a somewhat worldly way; they are not viewed with horror, nor are they seen as revealing some fundamental flaw in the society. The conflicts simply exist; but they can be tamed, thanks to the scope afforded in a free society to sensible institutions like formal bargaining procedures, arbitration and so on. The conflicts are seen as capable of being contained by rules, and it is considered rather important that they be so. The consequences of a lack of regulation, of conflict being allowed to become endemic, are believed to be chaos (Flanders and Fox, 1969). This essentially ethical rather than scientific aspect of the theory was openly stated by Clegg in a notable reply to his radical and Marxist critics (Clegg, 1975).

The stress on rules should not be confused with a belief in the efficacy of formal law. The emphasis placed on the importance of practices emerging on the shop floor and then being incorporated by union organizations leads most members of the industrial-relations school to be wary of the dangers of distorting the emergent processes by legal imposition from outside. There is considerable optimism over the capacity of free institutions to adapt and provide an adequate framework of rules if nudged and prompted by governments and managers – but not if forced by law, which is regarded as a crude instrument:

> But the case for preserving as much as we can of this aspect of voluntarism does not rest solely on grounds of social expediency. It finds its strongest defence in the very character of the human and social problems which industry creates.... The fact that industrial activity changes day by day, that technology and markets are constantly in flux, means that it cannot be directed with a sensitive regard for the manifold and diverse interests of those involved by a regime of strict external law and outside regulation.... Since we have no objective or socially agreed yardsticks to settle these questions they are best decided – within such limits as the public interest may impose – to the satisfaction of those who are most directly and intimately affected. This can only be done by representatives of their own choosing.... [Flanders, 1970: 177]

Or, as the Royal Commission on Trade Unions and Employers' Associations (1968a: para 475) put it, dealing with its preference for voluntary action prodded by government encouragement:

> As we found when seeking to identify the underlying causes of unofficial strikes, the root of the evil is in our present methods of collective bargaining and especially our methods of workshop bargaining, and it is in the absence of speedy, clear and effective disputes procedures. Until this defect is remedied, all attempts to make procedure agreements legally binding are bound to defeat themselves.

If institutions bound the world of this science, then

changes in institutions will be seen as capable of changing behaviour. For example, in the late 1960s, when there were strong signs that the autonomy of shop-floor power in many industries was threatening the capacity of formal unions to incorporate workers' power within a system of rules, the proposals of the institutional pluralists were, as indicated in the above quotations, for reforms in collective-bargaining practice (Flanders, 1965 and 1967; Royal Commission, 1968a). If the bargaining institutions adapted to allow formal participation by shop stewards, rather than keeping them on the margins of legitimacy, then their actions would become incorporated in the rule-governed system. But, argued the school's critics, if the stewards become incorporated, would not the workers simply turn to different representatives? If one of the workers' objectives in turning to the stewards rather than to the formal union officials was to avoid incorporation into formal procedure, there was little point in prescribing incorporation of the stewards. There was some evidence for this criticism in research carried out in the motor industry (Turner *et al.*, 1967: 222–9). This showed that in many cases shop stewards, committed to a bargaining machinery which they had helped to establish, were opposed to unofficial strikes that took place despite that machinery. The authors of this study distinguished between 'official-unofficial' strikes and 'unofficial-unofficial' ones, a designation implying a constant search by workers for escape from incorporation and commitment.

There is, therefore, in the approach of the institutional pluralists a major testable hypothesis: to what extent do changes in institutional structures change behaviour? The question remains unresolved. Examples such as that from the motor industry can be countered by those which seem to support the hypothesis. For example, in the late 1960s and early 1970s there was something of a militant shop-floor movement in certain sections of German industry. An Act of 1972 greatly extended the size and powers of the works councils – elected committees of workers which have legal rights to decide some issues and jointly agree others with management representatives in the conduct of German enterprises. The increase in the size of the councils enabled some of the emerging leaders of the shop-floor movement to be elected as members of them, while the increase in powers gave the councils greater ability to tackle workers' grievances. Apart from isolated areas, there has subsequently been some decline in the unofficial movement (Streeck, 1980).

Examples never clinch arguments. How does one know that the legal changes had anything to do with the change in behaviour of German workers? And even if they did, there may have been special factors influencing the case. But the example does suggest that the issue remains open; the scope for change induced by institutional changes should not be dismissed out of hand. It is probably time that the debate over this issue moved from the level of theory to an attempt to appraise the impact of a variety of cases of institutional innovation.

In the absence of such a test, there remain some further debates at the theoretical level. Even though institutional changes may be capable of inducing change in behaviour, the institutional school is vulnerable to criticism on the grounds that it limits its attention to these rather formal variables when analysing trade-union and other industrial-relations questions. For example, Clegg's (1976) comparison of different national industrial-relations systems seeks explanations of national differences almost solely in terms of variables included in industrial-relations machinery. Where, as in his discussion of political action and the state (ch. 8), some sense of the different roles of different states in the process of industrialization might have helped him, he falls back instead on ill-defined 'national attitudes'.

Against these criticisms the institutionalists claim, with some but not total success, that containment of a field of explanation by limiting the number of variables considered is essential if any serious testing of hypotheses is to be achieved (Clegg, 1979: 451). And they can point in support to the hopelessly general nature of much sociological work which tries to embrace the widest possible range of variables.

Another characteristic of this school's work which helps define its terms of reference and also generates criticism is its closeness to practice. As individuals, many senior members of this school serve governments, employers and unions, and much of their work is directed at policy-makers at various levels. American industrial-relations specialists have been subjected to strong and trenchant criticism on these grounds, being dubbed 'servants of power' (Baritz, 1960). It has been alleged that, by allowing so much of their work to be carried out on commission for industrial management, they have distorted their theories and research so that they respond to the problematics of a particular social group rather than to critieria of scientific enquiry. The same charge cannot so justifiably be made in this country: research carried out in the British academic tradition is usually somewhat more removed from the pressing concerns of extra-academic groups, there being far less unmediated industrial sponsorship of research; further, British industrial-relations specialists have been more even-handed in the 'sides' for which they work when they have undertaken outside commissions. While the biggest money may come from employers, many researchers have, for personal reasons, been politically sympathetic to trade unions.[2] This has helped produce healthily balanced research.

Nevertheless, the more subtle aspects of the argument can be applied to some British industrial-relations scholarship. In 1965 a Royal Commission on Trade Unions and Employers' Associations was established under the chairmanship of Lord Donovan. Its purpose was to examine the effectiveness of industrial-relations institutions, with particular attention to the scope to be afforded the law in regulating industrial relations. The Commission sponsored a good deal of research, and one of the consequences of its work was that government decided to support far more industrial-relations research thereafter. In particular,

the Social Science Research Council's Industrial Relations
Research Unit was established at the University of
Warwick in the post-Donovan period, and much of the best
research on the subject has come from that source.

The main aim of many employer-representatives who
appeared before Donovan was to have several measures of
legal regulation of trade-union activity advocated by the
Commission (Royal Commission, 1965a, 1966a, b, c,
1968b). Naturally, the unions opposed this. Most, though
not all, of the industrial-relations specialists who gave
evidence to Donovan took a similar line because of their
view that industrial relations developed best through
emergent properties rather than external imposition. They
therefore spoke favourably of free collective bargaining and
its capacity for internal voluntary reform (*ibid.*, 1965b,
1966d, e, f). While these beliefs and arguments existed
before Donovan, the work of the Commission led to some
major elaborations of this philosophy and, almost accident-
ally, equipped the subsequently expanding industrial-relations research activity with a set of deeply rooted concerns.
It is interesting to speculate whether the preoccupations of
the subject would be the same had the Donovan episode not
taken place.

Radicals

As has been noted, the institutional pluralist school takes
existing institutions for granted, and views employers and
workers (or unions) as constituting two 'sides' in a more or
less balanced struggle. It is this which has been criticized
by those I have called here the 'radical' school. Goldthorpe
(1974: 212–13), a major example of this school, commenting on the Donovan Report, asserted:

> Because the starting point is with industrial relations
> problems, which are taken as indicating some failure of
> regulative institutions, there is little concern to go, as it were,
> behind these problems and to enquire into the social

relationships and modes of action *which throw strain on such institutions* in the first place; that is, which create, and express, social conflict. Nowhere in the Donovan Report, or in the entire tradition of industrial relations writing on which it drew so heavily, is there to be found any systematic consideration of how the functioning of the economic system as a whole and of its constituent units of production is founded upon, and sustains, vast differences in social power and advantage; nor of how there are then generated – in undoubtedly complex ways – on the one hand, objective oppositions of interest, and, on the other, subjective responses of frustration, resentment and antagonism, and also in some degree aspirations and movements towards an alternative dispensation. [Original italics]

Alan Fox (1974a and b) distinguished the pluralist and radical approaches in similar terms. His position is particularly interesting in that he was for several years one of the pluralist school, and had, only a few years previously (1966), set out that school's standpoint as contrasted with the 'unitary' school in a document prepared for the Donovan Commission (1966). Indeed, in the wake of the Commission's Report he had been co-author, with Alan Flanders, of a paper (1969) which remains the main example of industrial-relations specialists going directly to classical sociology. They turned to the work of Emile Durkheim to interpret British industrial-relations problems as essentially those of a failure of *normative* framework. However, by 1974 Fox was writing:

Unlike the pluralist, however, the radical does not see the collective organization of employees into trade unions as restoring a balance of power (or anything as yet approaching it) between the propertied and the propertyless. He may well agree that it mitigates the imbalance and thereby enables employees to challenge some kinds of management decision on issues of special and immediate importance for them. But a great imbalance remains, symptomized by the fact that there are many other types of management decision which employees might aspire to influence were they conscious of having the power to do so, but from which they are presently completely excluded. [1974b: 15]

In calling proponents of these criticisms 'radical' one is not referring to their political beliefs, but to their intellectual approach – though the latter does sometimes imply the former. What is radical is the determination of this school to dig deeper into the social structure for its explanatory variables; it does not remain at the level of the explicitly industrial-relations institutions, nor does it take for granted the character of industrial conflict. Attention is instead directed at the abiding inequalities of the employment relationship, which leads the radicals to stress the endemic nature of conflict and the fact that its sources lie beyond the reach of institutional tinkering.

Another important characteristic of this school is its concern with workers' attitudes, frameworks of action, ideologies. Examining the industrial world from such a perspective often provides an account which contrasts sharply with those of conventional wisdom. Thus, Goldthorpe (1974: 197–8), commenting on the perplexity often expressed as to why workers seem to prefer a combination of time-wasting during the day with long hours of overtime to a short but intensive working day, argues that not only does the latter require workers to raise the intensity of their effort, but it also underestimates 'the possibility that time-wasting at the employer's expense may in itself be gratifying to workers'. Taking Flanders to task for saying that to take such a view implies a cynical view of humanity, he continues that workers in modern industrial enterprises:

. . . do often view their relationship with their employing organization in essentially calculative, 'money for effort' terms. Where this is so, it would then seem perfectly understandable that, under certain conditions, they might prefer to gain a certain level of earnings through a longer period of effort rather than through a shorter period of higher effort. . . . Furthermore, there is also extensive evidence of workers' concern to maintain their autonomy in the performance of their work tasks and roles and, to this end, to exert control of their own over basic features of the work situation – control over *time* being seen in various ways as highly important . . . it is not difficult to appreciate that being able to apply such control *against* management could be found inherently rewarding. In addition, in the particular instance of time-wasting, it needs also to be appreciated that 'time out' may sometimes serve a significant social function for the work group; that is, it may provide opportunity for various activities through which the solidarity of the group, and the shared beliefs and values of its members, are daily reinforced. [p. 198]

This kind of work is very much from the heartland of modern British sociology as it has developed over the past twenty years or more. Its theoretical base has been established by such writers as John Rex (1961) and David Lockwood (1956). They have depicted society as an arena within which social actors (individuals as well as groups) pursue conflicting goals according to various beliefs about means and ends. These beliefs constitute their ideology or consciousness, though these writers, unlike phenomenologists and ethnomethodologists, never lose sight of the fact that a rational calculation of advantage in a context of real power relations is always at stake. Few prior assumptions are made about the identity of institutions, which are contingent on action, and virtually no assumptions are made about the contours of the overall system; indeed, a lot of energy has been devoted to demolishing the very concept of an elaborated social system, especially as it had been presented in the works of Talcott Parsons. Certainly there are no assumptions that mechanisms exist in society to check and absorb conflict; rather, the society is seen as shot through with potential conflicts as different groups of actors pursue mutually incompatible goals. These authors have something in common with Marxist writers in their emphasis on the continuous possibilities for conflicts of interests, but do not agree that these conflicts always concern *class* interests (Parkin, 1979).

This approach, stressing the subjective states of social actors and the effects these states have on structuring their pursuit of frequently conflicting goals, is not the only way of doing sociology; I have already noted that the industrial-relations institutional school tends, indirectly, to draw on the work of Parsons, whose structural functionalism is very different. But it is the approach which predominates among British sociologists, whether they are studying industrial relations or other social phenomena.

Another characteristic of this school is, in contrast with the institutionalists, its lack of involvement in practical consultancy or policy-making. While this is in no way related to the previous point about theory, the two characteristics combine to give the work of this school a very non-committal character. It tends to correct or adjust popular conceptions (either by empirical refutation or by critical argument), and to point to the folly of superficial institutional tinkering, but then stands back, rarely asserting any positive positions about the nature of trade-union activity (see the exchange between Goldthorpe and certain economists on the related question of sociologists' attitude to inflation, in Hirsch and Goldthorpe, 1978: 214–16).

Marxists

Finally, there are the Marxists. There are many different strands of Marxism within and around sociology, partly because we are here dealing with a political movement as much as an academic school, with elements of theory being treated more as articles of faith than as items of imperfect and contingent knowledge; and partly because Marxism, as a 'rebel' movement, always outside the academic establishment, is particularly vulnerable to swings of transitory fashion. But behind all the differences certain major features unite most Marxists and distinguish them from many other scholars in the field.

If the radicals were differentiated from the institutional pluralists by their digging deeper into the social structure to find their explanatory variables, the Marxists take this process further. The cornerstone of Marxist analysis is the identification of the class relationship between capital and labour as the major determinant of social relations, the major explanation of why social actors behave the way they do or of why particular institutions exist (Hyman, 1975: 17–23 and ch. 4). The endemic conflicts of capitalist society are, for Marxists, essentially class conflicts; and the motor of social change is the working out of the contradictions inherent in a class society. From that perspective any social explanation that does not reduce its variables to class terms, but spends time on intermediate factors without tracing them back to class, is inadequate. Something of the flavour of this standpoint is captured in the critique of Fox's radicalism offered by Wood and Elliott (1977). They claim that, while Fox uses a Marxist framework in order to criticize Clegg and other pluralists, when he comes himself to propose changes he assumes the possibility of gradual social improvements which maintain the divide between managers and managed. Indeed, they consider that his approach to change assumes that employers (the dominant class) will be willing to carry out reforms; his stress on 'trust' relations between managers and employees is 'con-servative ... elitist and technocratic' (*ibid*: 115). His approach is therefore not really much different from that of the pluralists, as he believes in the 'mutual survival' of antagonistic class interests (p. 114).

Fox, replying to this criticism (1979), claimed that Wood and Elliott had misrepresented his theory at certain points. In particular, the argument that he saw all change as coming from management was based on just one essay of his, which happened to have been directed specifically at a managerial audience (Fox, 1974b); in his work as a whole he had by no means taken the view that reforms always proceeded from the top – very much the reverse. More important, he distinguished between a 'commitment to liberal pluralism' (i) which meant believing that countries like Britain, with deep social inequalities, *were* already adequately liberal and pluralist, and (ii) that which meant that one believed in the values of liberal pluralism as a means of action and a desirable goal. The fact that he held to (ii) did not imply that he believed (i). Indeed, he continued, it was the association of Marxism with blanket attacks on any kind of liberal pluralism that led many people to believe that Marxists were actually opposed to liberal and pluralist values in principle – a factor which then led them to reject even the valid insights of Marxist analysis.

Marxists differ among themselves, but several of them would respond to Fox's counterattack by saying that yes, they did reject liberal pluralism as a value and not just as a professed description of fact; that the pluralism that 'balances' a dominant management and a subservient workforce can never be a genuine pluralism; and that there could be a true liberation of the workers only when that very difference between employer- and employee-interests that rests at the heart of pluralism was destroyed in revolutionary struggle. There are, then, various Marxist answers to the question of what will replace the division between managers and managed, and how pluralism among different interests within the workforce will be expressed if the emphasis of the labour movement has hitherto been placed on a monolithic struggle between the massed forces of capital and labour. These answers have to find their own solution to the fact that, to date, all cases of successful revolutions carried out in the name of Marx have replaced the division between capitalist managers and workers with one between state managers and workers, and have rejected all subsequent expressions of dissent and conflict among workers.

This is a subject to which we shall return, but it is not the end of the problems of Marxist analysis. While trade unionism seems an obvious subject for a Marxist approach, it does in fact present great difficulties for Marxist theory – difficulties which date back to Marx's own relations with trade unionists in nineteenth-century Britain. On the one hand, unions are (or seem to be) an expression of class conflict, of workers' dissatisfaction with capitalist society.

But trade unionism tries to resolve workers' grievances *within* the employment relationship: it looks for concessions and improvements from the capitalists and stops short of revolutionary activity (Hyman, 1975: ch. 3). Orthodox Marxist theory of early twentieth-century communist parties solved the problem this way: the unions were useful for an initial mobilization of the working class, but, after a point, workers with revolutionary potential had to move on to activity within the communist party to become true revolutionaries. Thus, in the evocative phrase of French communists, the union serves as a 'conveyor belt' for the party, bringing workers out of the mass of the apathetic and delivering them to the party. But in practice that kind of relationship always causes problems for unions. The union becomes severely subordinate to the party, rarely daring to take up issues without party guidance for fear that it might overstep its prescribed role. Thus Lenin had very little use for trade unions, either in his political writings or in his practical activity (see Hyman, 1971: 26–8); free trade unions did not long survive the Russian Revolution, but were absorbed and refashioned by the Bolshevik Party, which was by then almost synonymous with the state. Subsequently, no trade-union movement has maintained its autonomy from the state following a communist takeover of government. It is notable that the only significant autonomous union to be founded within a communist society, the Polish union Solidarity, is not Marxist and has very difficult relations with the Marxist Polish state. In societies with large but unsuccessful communist parties, their associated union movements have become notorious for their incapacity to respond alertly to workers' demands without reference to the party. Such was for a long time the position in Italy, and still is in France (Dubois *et al.*, 1978; Reynaud, 1975).

The historical background for the Marxist study of trade unions is therefore not as encouraging as might be supposed. However, over the past two decades or so, certain changes have taken place. First, disillusion with the Soviet

Union following repeated evidence of its internal brutality, from the invasion of Hungary in 1956 onwards, led to the desertion of the communist party in Britain and other European countries by many political activists who still found themselves on the left of established labour and social democratic parties, and who set about forming and joining small Trotskyist and other groups. The intellectuals of these movements were now freed from doctrines of the central role of the party. Second, from the 1960s on, and especially from around 1968, shop-floor militancy became increasingly important as an industrial phenomenon, and, given government involvement in incomes policies, as a political phenomenon too. Left-wing intellectuals were able to embrace this development without the constraints and ambiguities of orthodox communists, and saw in it the new social force from which a revolutionary transformation of society might spring. From this essentially political concern has come a stream of writing and research which has often considerably increased our knowledge of union activity and workers' militancy on the shop floor (for the clearest statements of the case, see Allen [1966] and Hyman [1971]).

But these writers retain the problem encountered by Marx, Lenin and other previous generations of Marxist observers of trade unions: however militant their action, unions (including shop-floor groups) usually stop short at 'economistic' demands which lead them into compromises with management. But where the Leninists sought a solution to this difficulty by stressing the role of the party, present observers have learned the lessons of this and look instead to the potentiality for revolutionary consciousness in individual workers: the constant search for evidence of revolutionary beliefs among workers, and the incessant return to the question: why do the workers not revolt? As will be discussed in chapter 4, there is much naivety in this expectation that there might exist a fully worked-out intellectual ideology in the minds of masses of ordinary working men; there was a robust realism in Lenin's acceptance that revolutionary consciousness was likely to be a minority pursuit, and that that minority would have to form a vanguard within the party leadership, whose mission was to act as the consciousness of the whole class. (What he ignored – and this will be a theme of chapter 5 – was the consequent problem of power within the organizations of the labour movement.) As a result of this search for revolutionary consciousness, much Marxist literature contains a vain glorification of temporary incidents of revolt, such as when a few workers at Vauxhall Motors, in a burst of anger, wrecked some managerial offices;[3] or of acts of sabotage and horseplay that disrupt industrial production (e.g., Beynon, 1973: ch. 6). But among the more serious Marxist researchers a genuine enquiry into these same questions which have been called naive here can produce interesting results, for they sometimes seek to understand why non-revolutionary workers do have the beliefs they hold. A good example is Nichols and Armstrong's (1976) study of a deliberately selected group of non-militant workers:

Committed socialists will hardly help to advance the low level of organization and consciousness characteristic of firms like ChemCo if they pretend the men employed in them are already engaged in a battle over control when, collectively, they are not. No real movement for greater control is going to be helped, either, by a failure to acknowledge that ambivalent though their feelings may be, workers, like many of those at ChemCo, know they indisputably have real interests in continuing their present employment – and also face very real problems in further control at local level. The fact they have such problems may serve to underline the necessity for political action. But to say this is to define what part of the problem is. To find an answer to the problem is, to put it modestly, rather more difficult. [p. 83]

This kind of work really teaches us something about the nature and problems of workers' collective action. Further, since a preoccupation with workers' subjective beliefs and attitudes already characterizes orthodox sociology, as we have seen above, it can be readily assimilated into the general corpus of sociological knowledge.

But not all Marxist contributions concentrate on subjective perceptions. Recently, several Marxist scholars have returned to an earlier tradition of Marxist study: attention to the underlying economic processes of capitalist society. It is central to Marxist social theory that capitalism is inherently unstable and that, as capitalists try to preserve their system, so they only worsen its internal contradictions and bring about its eventual demise. The search for the mechanisms through which these contradictions work themselves out provides the subject for Marxist scholarship in this area. Trade unions are not necessarily at the centre of such a study. In Marx's own classical formulation of the issue, the core of the capitalist crisis lay in the process of capitalist competition and accumulation itself. In the drive to compete with each other for markets, capitalists would be forced to cut production costs by installing more machinery and reducing the labour content of their production methods. However, given Marx's theory that all profit derived from extracting a surplus from the deployment of labour power, reducing the proportion of labour employed must reduce capitalists' rate of profit. The results of competition are, in his view, a reduction in profits, which the capitalists try to recoup by forcing down wages, pressing workers ever closer to the subsistence line. It is as workers resist this process and are spurred to anger by it that they develop organizations to help wage the struggle – organizations which eventually become a political fighting force for directing the revolutionary struggle. While workers' organizations play a crucial role in this process, it is clearly secondary. It is not the strength of union action as such which provokes the crisis.

Many Marxist theoreticians maintain similar views today, but the palpable rise in union power in past decades has led others to ascribe a higher place to workers' action in provoking as well as responding to the capitalist crisis. For example, in a widely noted work, two Marxist economists developed the thesis that the success of British union action in winning wage increases was squeezing capitalist profits and thereby helping to cause the crisis of British capitalism (Glyn and Sutcliffe, 1972) – a view shared in some respects by many British employers, as the authors acknowledge:

> ... the fall in the profitability of capital, in an internationally competitive atmosphere, has been greatly accelerated by working-class wage pressure. This may make it sound as though we are arguing on the side of capital against the workers. After all, capitalists always say they cannot afford to pay higher wages. But our findings ought to strengthen and not weaken the working class if they are interpreted in the right way. We have shown that capitalism will be unable to continue accepting the rate of wage increase which has prevailed in the recent past without jeopardizing its own existence. This means that the working-class leaders must adopt a new attitude to wage demands: they must realize that wage claims are becoming political weapons in a battle in which the existence of capitalism is at stake. [p. 212]

Glyn and Sutcliffe are economists. Within the Marxist tradition their work is compatible with that of more sociological writers who have tried to demonstrate the precise ways in which workers' action produces contradictions for capitalism. Thus Hyman (1975: 104) argues that certain issues are incapable of being contained within an orthodox bargaining framework:

> The specific features of employment instability are manifest in the displacement of established industries and occupations.... Redundancy has become an everyday feature of contemporary British capitalism; so have speed-up and other forms of work intensification for workers who do retain their jobs. Thus despite the pressure towards trade union economism, conflict is inevitably generated over questions of conditions and control. Indeed, as the most basic element of job control – whether a particular job is to exist at all – assumes central importance, so the viability of purely fragmented struggle is eroded; it is impossible successfully to combat the employer at the point of production, if his intention is in fact to *cease* production altogether. A campaign for the 'right to work' can only be effectively developed as a

general demand, with explicitly political and not merely economic implications.

If, as now seems to be the case, issues of this kind grow in importance, the possibilities of rising, endemic and increasingly politicized conflict become very real. Hyman does, however, evade the question whether the demand implicit in this passage – that everyone should have the right to retain indefinitely his or her existing job – is realizable under any foreseeable social order.

Clearly it is important to the Marxist view that nothing impede the prosecution of conflicts which will worsen the condition of capitalism to the point of collapse (the question, which Marx himself asked, whether 'socialism or barbarism' would follow such a collapse, is, rather surprisingly, only rarely ventilated). It follows that Marxists are highly critical of institutions designed to lessen the intensity of conflict: forms of mediation and arbitration, rules for regulating disputes, even trade-union leaderships. The study of the way in which such institutions frustrate and betray workers' struggles thus provides another subject for Marxist enquiry. Here again, an essentially political inspiration has led to research projects which have in fact told us a good deal about the ways in which these institutions work:

> ... the state has also been called upon to set a legal and administrative framework for the peaceful settlement of disputes between employers and workers. These arrangements are of indubitable benefit to capital, whose profits depend on normal continuity of production. They have no such certain advantage for labour, except on the assumption that private appropriation of profit is as sacrosanct as state-encouraged collective bargaining assumes it to be. Unions cannot negotiate to abolish profit: it is on that unspoken premise that the wheels of conflict resolution in industrial relations turn.... Even when the refrain of public policy is conciliation rather than confrontation ... it is conciliation always on terms that take the maintenance of private profit for granted. Whatever the pay-off for labour, it is within those fixed limits.
> [Westergaard and Resler, 1975: 199]

But whatever the value of Marxist contributions, they are marred by two crucial characteristics: the assumption that all issues can be reduced to those of capital and labour, and the search for revolutionary consciousness. The latter will be pursued in chapter 4. As to the former, the reminder that the capital-labour conflict is central to industrial relations is important; it is a point usually ignored by the institutional school, and subsequent chapters will show that it is important to my own analysis. But to reduce everything to class is highly misleading. For example, the perplexing fact that many industrial disputes take the form of one group of workers insisting on earning a certain percentage more than another group of workers is sometimes resolved by Marxists by claiming that, since it is capital which defines different categories of workers, and since the wage demand is in fact made against the employer, disputes about differentials of this kind are really struggles between capital and labour (Hyman, 1975: 17–23). The problem with the first part of this argument is that it assumes that, in the absence of private ownership of the means of production, there would be no division of labour; or that workers would cease to care about their relative standing. These are such large claims that they go beyond the bounds of even potentially available knowledge and cannot be used to support an argument. The problem with the second part is that it assumes that, were there to be no capitalist employer, there need be no limits to the realization of pay claims; which is clearly untrue.[4] While capital certainly represents a class interest, the limitations on workers' pursuit of higher wages which the capitalist employer enforces are also determined by factors other than the capitalist's profit level, such as the unwillingness of consumers to pay indefinitely increasing sums for goods and services. Identification of the class interests at stake certainly gives us a deeper level of analysis than formal institutions, but it is not always, as Marxists claim (Hyman and Brough, 1975: 167), the final analysis. Behind class interests stands the general human problem of the scarcity of desired resources.

To take another example, Clarke and Clements, in a recent work on *Trade Unions under Capitalism* (1977), refer to the contention expressed by a colleague, Huw Beynon, that capitalism is the cause of most of the problems experienced by industrial workers:

> In response to a demand by a senior academic that technology was the determining factor in the high level of alienation and conflict experienced in the motor industry, Beynon once disturbed the sacrosanct air of a post-graduate seminar with the retort, 'No! It's not technology – it's fucking capitalism!' It is, perhaps, regrettable that the rigorous candour of his analysis is rare in academic discussion. The determinism of those who view technological development as a neutral impersonal force ignores the human agency and interests involved in such processes, and the power relations which determine their outcome.... [p. 226]

The final point is well taken, but an objection remains. If it is capitalism, however adjectivally qualified, which is the cause of alienation and conflict, why are the levels of those phenomena not uniformly high in all industries? This is a pertinent question if the point at issue is, as seems to have been the case in Beynon's discussion, the distinctively high levels in the motor industry. Glossing over this kind of point does little credit to Marxist analyses.

Conclusion

I have drawn attention to the strengths and weaknesses of the three schools I have identified. This book belongs essentially in the second group, the 'radicals', or at least it can be designated such with no more injustice to individual differences than has been done to the many other people here so roughly allocated to categories. The approach of the radicals, by seeking explanations in terms of the wider social structure rather than those limited to the immediate institutional structure of industrial relations, is more satisfactory than that of the institutional pluralists, while its conception of that social structure is more subtle and complex, less dogmatic, than that which lends an air of unreality to much Marxist analysis. However, in this work I am trying to remedy what I see as one of the defects of the radical or sociological school, its lack of a theoretical statement on trade unionism. In order to do this, I shall to some extent depart from one of the central attributes of the school: its concern with workers' *subjective* perceptions and attitudes. This is not because I regard that concern as unimportant or wrong, but because *preoccupation with it has directed our attention away from the scope for abstract assumptions of rationality in workers' conduct.*

The action frame of reference is in fact well suited to rational accounts. It assumes actors with goals which they seek to realize through certain available means and in relationships with other social actors whose own pursuit of goals either reinforces or conflicts with the attempts of the original actors. Once we start specifying goals and means we can begin to make theories about the ways actors are likely to act. Part of the context in which the actors work will be provided by their subjective values and perceptions, so this kind of approach fits very well with the action framework. However, there is a tendency for sociology to place such stress on this factor that it ignores a crucial aspect of human goal-seeking behaviour: the need to make constant *choices* about which means to adopt, or about the priority to be accorded different goals, or about the best means of treating conflict and obstacles. Social action can be seen as a mass of choices, each of which involves a calculation of gain and loss. This is the view of life which is central to the discipline of economics and it has helped economists to make a good deal of progress in predicting and explaining behaviour. As we must expect, the choice to fashion their discipline that way has involved a cost for economists. In order to build abstract models about the kinds of choices actors are likely to make, they have to make assumptions about the identity of goals and about actors' determination to maximize the goals they seek. These may not be realistic assumptions; in practice many people may not, for example, try to maximize their goals. To base their theories on people's actually observed motivations would add to the realism of economists' explanations, but it would limit their ability to construct theoretical systems.

Much current British sociology seems to have made the opposite choice, being concerned with what people 'really' think and believe at the expense of theory construction (Hyman and Brough, 1975: 129–34). This also directs attention away from the rationale of choice. For example, if a sociologist is asked to give an account of why a group of workers chose to strike or not to strike over a particular grievance, he is likely to answer in terms of the beliefs of the workers – such as their perception of the legitimacy of the employer's power (for a good example, see Eldridge and Cameron, 1964). An economist is more likely to look at the cost of striking to the workers, set against the gains they might be expected to achieve from the action. Neither approach is more correct than the other; they are complementary. But I want in the succeeding chapters to redress the balance in modern sociology's treatment, exploring the scope for a sociological theory of trade unionism cast in a model of rational action, but, I hope, without losing touch with that concern both for relevant social questions and for the importance of subjective attitudes on which sociologists so rightly insist.

Being true to a rational-choice approach, I cannot pretend that I can maximize two such goals without cost. The cost will be that the discussion remains elementary, introductory and at times undeveloped. To illustrate further this choice, I would cite the criticism of Dunlop's (1944) economistic account of wage determination launched by A. M. Ross (1948) and pursued more recently by Atherton (1973). Though economists, these critics want to go further in their theory of unionism than the trade-off which unions must make between wages and the level of employment, and consider what they describe as unions' 'political' goals as well. By this Ross meant maintaining the union organization and the position of its leadership within it; Atherton meant a union's goal of maximizing its membership. In so doing they advance the theory of union behaviour considerably. But is internal organization and maximizing membership what most of us understand by the phrase 'unions' political goals'? What about unions' attempts to alter the wage-employment relationship by affecting government economic policy? What about the diversion of their energies from wage goals to, say, lobbying for increased retirement pensions from the state? These are the issues which I shall discuss when I reach the chapter on political aspects of union work (chapter 6); but given such broad themes I shall be unable to achieve anything like the rigour of analysis of Ross's or Atherton's accounts.

Within sociology the approach I am adopting is usually known as exchange theory (because of the exchange of costs for benefits almost universally involved in a rational approach to action) or, more accurately, as rational-choice theory.[5] Unfortunately, many of the practitioners of such theory have, in trying to rival the precision of economists' models, reduced the variables they discuss until their accounts have an irritating lack of realism. Also, less excusably, they often tend to relate the rational choices to the dilemmas of *individual* actors, and their work rapidly becomes a form of psychology. This is unnecessary, since the point of a sociological approach to rational choice and exchange is precisely to investigate how the logic of human conduct is affected by the essentially *collective* nature of much of that conduct.

The central characteristics, and usefulness, of the approach can be seen when we consider various ways of answering the question 'Why?' when addressed to any particular social action or series of actions. For example, why did a particular group of workers join trade unions while another group did not? Why did the mineworkers strike in 1974 but not in 1980? Why have workers in the engineering industry been very successful in securing control over immediate working methods, but very unsuccessful in affecting investment decisions by their employers? In each case the rational-choice approach asks: what were the actors' chances of success in attaining a particular goal? What did it cost them to take action towards attaining it? What alternatives presented themselves, and what were the associated risks and costs of them? To what extent did the actors' chosen course conflict with those of other actors, and what sanctions did each bring to bear against the other? What knowledge was available to the actors about all these facts?

Such an approach differs from, for example, one which immediately explains action in terms of ideology, consciousness or imagery; or from one which makes inferences from the structure of relations between social actors without examining the implications of that structure for behaviour. As we shall see, rational-choice accounts cannot ignore social perceptions or consciousness, but they will not accept them as the automatic (and, indeed, frequently tautological) explanations of human conduct. They will also be interested in structural imbalances in social relations, such as the fundamental inequality between capital and labour. But rather than merely asserting this, rational-choice accounts will try to show precisely how that imbalance enters into the pattern of action chosen by the different social actors.[6] While some writers in this tradition may have lost the idea of power within the notion of exchange, many others have been very alive to the possibility of highly unequal exchange, an approach which in fact proves a very useful way of tackling the difficult question of assessing power. I hope to demonstrate this in subsequent chapters, but the point has been particularly well made in Blau's *Exchange and Power in Social Life* (1964).

However, rational-choice theories also need to be distinguished from the behavioural school of industrial relations (for an outline of which, see Margerison, 1969). This concentrates on details of the actual conduct of participants in particular situations, such as the goals of managers and union representatives or the style of their contact. This leads to a similar form of account to that given in the following chapters, the difference being one of focus and distance. In looking at particular cases and the precise factors that produce specific outcomes, behavioural theory can be very helpful. But if one is interested in broader, more generalizable determinants of action, it can leave us with an unwieldy number of variables. It is an example of the familiar difference between the study of woods and that of trees: if we concentrate on the details of individual trees, we may forget that they are part of a wood, though that does not mean that the study of woods is always more appropriate than that of trees.

The main defect of an economic approach is that it reduces the complexity of social values to a simple assumption of the pursuit of rational self-interest. Nevertheless, this defect has its advantages. The assumption of a calculative pursuit of self-interest does make it possible to construct advanced theories of how people will act, on which predictions can be based; and these predictions can be seen to be more or less accurate in their outcome. If they prove accurate, well and good; if they are frequently inaccurate, we can always re-examine our basic assumptions about motives. But even if calculative self-interest seems a poor guide, we do well not to relinquish the general assumption of rationality or self-interest; we can regard the motivations which seem to contradict this motive as limitations imposed on the extent of the rationality, or as constraints within which the rationality has to operate, and, having adjusted our theory, we can start again to make predictions based on rational self-interest. This is an approach often favoured by anthropologists, who wish to avoid the assumption that behaviour in, say, tribal societies is in some sense irrational (Horton, 1967). For example, a particular tribe may refuse to eat meat, even though that is the only food available for them, because they believe that meat-eating offends the gods. This may seem to be a departure from calculative self-interest. But is it? If we temporarily assume their belief about the anger of the gods to be correct, surely we have to agree with them that the consequences of offending supernatural beings may well be far worse than the consequences of starving to death. Within the constraints imposed by their belief system they are entirely rational, and predictions about their conduct can make use of rational-choice theory once we have accepted that constraint. There is still the larger question of whether it is rational to hold such a belief, and at what point we expect people to test the reliability of the knowledge on which they base their actions; but for some predictive purposes we are entitled to ignore this.

This example may seem a far cry from the problems we encounter in studying contemporary trade unions, but several of the points remain valid; by looking for different degrees of rationality, and for the constraints within which rational calculation operates, we are able to save something of the empirical richness which sociological and anthropological study of values and social imagery provides, while still retaining the hard base of calculative logic on the basis of which scientific prediction can be made.

2 The Drive to Combine

The most fundamental question in a study of trade unionism as rational action is: is it rational for workers to combine together in unions at all? The simplest answer is to point to the weakness of the isolated individual worker in his relations with his employer. While the labour contract pretends to be an even-handed relationship between two equal partners, this is purely a legal fiction. The individual employee is always precisely that, an individual man or woman; but the 'individual employer' is probably a company, including among its employees those working on problems of how to control labour and keep its costs down. But even the one-man business is backed by the capital invested in the plant, whereas the individual worker really is just himself. Combination appears as a rational strategy for workers because it offers the chance of reducing, though never of overcoming, this inequality. By standing together instead of alone they can threaten that, unless their conditions improve in various ways, they will ensure that no work goes on in the plant; they can develop an organization to look after their interests, which might in some respects rival the organization which the employer has to take care of his; and they may be able to prevent people from working in the firm at low rates of pay, thereby limiting the employer's ability to pick and choose in the labour market.

It is therefore in at least the medium-term interests of workers to combine. In the short term they may have problems because, if combination is likely to improve their position in relation to their employer, the employer is likely to place obstacles in their way. In the long term there may be problems in that success in raising the cost of labour to the firm may reduce the firm's competitiveness. This last argument will be taken up in a later chapter, since it is unlikely to affect the initial decision to combine, which is our present concern. The other problem, employer opposition, is, however, very relevant, because it involves the employer in so raising the cost of combination that workers dare not attempt it, despite the possibly large benefits which might be achieved from doing so.

Employer opposition has been of critical importance in trade-union history (Webb and Webb, 1920; Frow *et al.*, 1971). In the late eighteenth and early nineteenth centuries, when governments were in no way responsible to ordinary people, employers had little difficulty in gaining the support of governments in this task, and combinations of workers were often made illegal. In England, this took the form of the Combination Acts of 1799 and 1800 (repealed in 1824 and 1825). Similar legislation was enacted in post-revolutionary France and elsewhere. Punishments for attempting to form unions were often very severe.

Raising the cost of combination certainly had its effect, but it was never totally successful (Thompson, 1968: 543–69). In particular, groups of skilled craftsmen fought to retain their right to combine. That it was these better-off sections of the working class who did so can be explained, partly because the practice of skill gave these workers a sense of prestige and of solidarity with each other, but partly in terms of their high expectation of gains. Craftsmen had practised combination in the past, and they knew it helped to raise their wages and ensure for them unilateral control over how their work was carried out (Webb and Webb, 1920). In early industries the employer did not control and supervise every detail of work performance as is now the normal case, but hired gangs of craftsmen who then organized the work themselves. In the long run these workers won the right to legal combination, but lost unilateral job control; whether the latter made possible more efficient working methods which raised workers' wages is another and a difficult question to resolve. The winning of legal rights to organize came gradually as governments saw the likelihood of less social conflict if they permitted unions than if they tried to prevent them, and as they hastened to pursue policies that would attract political support from the rising number of manual workers who were achieving the suffrage during the latter part of the nineteenth century. Of course, the ending of the prohibition on unions did not end all obstacles to unionization; employers could continue to dismiss and otherwise harass workers who joined unions, and did so. But the fact that workers continued to fight such obstacles is an indication of the strength of the drive to combine, even if it was often a case of minorities of activists winning rights that all workers could subsequently enjoy.

These issues may seem to belong to the past of trade-union history; obstacles placed in the way of unionization apparently play little part in the calculations of modern workers considering whether or not to join a union. But this is not so. Opposition continues, sometimes just as crudely as in the past, but more often under different guises. One of the major changes currently taking place in the international economy is a shift in the locus of many manufacturing industries away from the old industrial heartlands of Europe and North America towards certain countries in the Third World known as the newly industrializing countries, in particular Taiwan, Hong Kong, South Korea, Singapore, Brazil, Colombia, South Africa (Fröbel *et al.*, 1977). Several factors explain this development, but one of them is the fact that nearly all these countries have dictatorial governments which either prohibit or severely limit the scope of trade unions. Workers in unionized Western industries are therefore confronted by competition from countries with poor working conditions and health and safety standards and low wages –

and, consequently, cheaper products. This may have important long-term consequences for the issue of trade-union membership; while the density of union membership has been rising in nearly all Western industrial countries during the past decade, if one takes the world as a whole it is likely that the overall proportion of industrial workers *throughout the world* who were members of, or even had the right to be members of, independent trade unions, has been declining.

If global developments of this kind seem rather remote, we may consider the case of the largest and most advanced industrial country of all: the United States of America. The continental scale of that country gives it some of the characteristics of the world as a whole, that is, the co-existence of old-established manufacturing regions with those where industrial development is only now progressing and replacing agricultural employment. And as is happening on a world scale, within the USA there is a shift in industrial employment from the unionized north-east to the newly developing south and west, where employers are fighting hard and ruthlessly to prevent their workers from joining unions. This process has been studied by Donald Roy (1980), who distinguishes three employer tactics, which he terms 'fear stuff, sweet stuff and evil stuff'. The first is the most obvious. Workers are made to fear the consequences of joining a union by punishments meted out to those who dare do so; they may be sacked, denied loans or other favours that workers might expect to receive from employers, denied promotion or the chances of better or more pleasant jobs, transferred to less convenient plants, given dirtier jobs or heavy workloads and refused wage increases – wage increases being on a more individual basis in the USA than in Britain. The entire workforce may also be threatened with closure or transfer of the plant or short-time working if they dare to join a union. 'Sweet stuff' is the strategy of providing a mass of benefits and sudden improvements in treatment to workers when a union recruiting drive is launched among them, leading the workers to consider union membership unnecessary – benefits which may well be removed once the recruiting drive has receded. 'Evil stuff' refers to what one might call 'black propaganda', the spreading of extraordinary rumours of the alleged dark deeds of unions. In the North American context, this will include allegations of communism and of anti-Christianity.

These activities have been assisted by expert advice from a number of sophisticated law firms and management consultants specializing in advising employers how to maintain a 'union-free plant'. Many of the advocates of this late twentieth-century drive against workers' ability to organize are prominent among the supporters of the current President of the USA, Ronald Reagan. During his administration something of this strategy has entered relations between government and its own employees, usually a field of fairly peaceful industrial relations. For example, in 1981 striking air-traffic controllers were sacked from their jobs, some were imprisoned and union officers fined; the government refused outright to negotiate with the controllers' union. It is ironic that Mr Reagan and his colleagues welcomed so effusively the emergence of free trade unions in Poland.

Even in the United Kingdom, where unions are well established and have recently acquired some legal safeguards for workers' rights to representation, when employers see the opportunity to exclude unions they often take it. The subtler forms of discrimination are found most often in white-collar employment, because it is there that employees' work is more likely to be of an individual nature, and assessment of their pay and prospects is more likely to be subject to individual decision-making by their employer. Manual workers are more likely to be treated as an undifferentiated mass; it is therefore interesting to learn that white-collar workers seem to depend, far more than do manual workers, on employer acceptance of union membership as an inducement to join; they are less likely to fight employers for the right. This is one of the explanations of the greater level of white-collar unionization in public than in private employment – the government as employer being committed to encouraging union membership among its employees:

> While employee concentration is a favourable condition for the growth of white-collar unions, it is not by itself sufficient. Employers must also be prepared to recognize these unions. The greater the degree to which employers are willing to do this, the more likely white-collar employees are to join unions. This is because they are less likely to jeopardize their career prospects by joining, they can more easily reconcile union membership with their 'loyalty' to the company, and they will obtain a better service as their unions will be more effective in the process of job regulation.
>   . . . The industrial strength of white-collar unions . . . has generally not been sufficient in itself to force employers to concede recognition. This has also required the introduction of government policies which have made it easier for unions to exert pressure for recognition and harder for employers to resist it. [Bain, 1970: 184]

These barriers are gradually being broken by unions, but the struggle continues in sectors which employ mainly female, foreign or seasonal labour, such as hotels and restaurants – for reasons which will be considered later. One such case in 1977 achieved considerable publicity. A group of primarily Asian workers, many of them women, at the Grunwick photo-processing works in North London demanded union representation, struck and were dismissed by their employer (Rogaly, 1977). The case achieved prominence because large numbers of supporters came to help the dismissed workers try to prevent work from continuing at the factory. The police arrived in similarly large numbers to assist the employer to keep his works open, and Conservative newspapers and politicians seized upon the employer as a hero in the struggle against trade unions. The dispute ended with the complete defeat of the workers. Such a case is important in demonstrating the high stakes involved in the struggle for union membership, the sacrifices people are sometimes willing to make to achieve it, and the lengths to which employers will go in trying to make the costs unacceptably high.

The problem of collective action

But employer opposition is not the only explanation of the failure of some groups of workers to form or join unions. If the potential gains from combination are as great as some seem to think, why does not every employee at least try to join? Union density in Britain is currently around 55 per cent of the labour force, and it has reached that level only in recent years. In some countries it is larger – in Sweden, an exceptional case, it is about 75 per cent – but in more it is much lower, in France being probably little more than 20 per cent. Within Britain the pattern is similarly varied; in some occupations, such as coal mining or the civil service, it is over 90 per cent, while in financial services it is about 20 per cent (though rising sharply). Further, if unionization is a means whereby workers can offset some of their weakness in the labour market, presumably the greatest gains are to be had by those weakest in the labour market; and yet we often find that these have the lowest levels of union membership. How are these facts to be explained? We have to go beyond general accounts of why unions are likely to exist, and explore why *individual* workers should want to join them.

To answer these questions we need to explore the rationality of trade-union membership, going beyond the most readily comprehensible point that combination would seem a rational aim for workers provided they can overcome any costs imposed by employer opposition. An important contribution to the study of the greater complexities was made by Mancur Olson in his study *The Logic of Collective Action* (1965), which dealt not just with trade unions, but with general problems of membership recruitment (and other acts of collectivism, such as voting) in large organizations devoted to providing public goods. A 'public' good here is one that is made generally available, that is, one does not need to be a member of the organization which provides the good to benefit from it. The problem is that the increase in the strength of the organization achieved by the addition of one more member is infinitesimal, whereas if one is a member of the wider community which the organization is trying to benefit, one will receive the benefits without needing to join. On the other hand, the costs of joining will be significant to the individual. On a rational cost/benefit calculation, the individual should therefore conclude that it is not worth joining the organization. To take an example outside industrial relations, let us consider the case of a national consumer organization which is, say, campaigning for improved safety in children's toys. As a parent of small children I might be expected to join the organization, because I share its goals. Not necessarily so, Olson would argue. Joining the organization will cost me money, and probably time and effort subsequently when participating in its campaigns. On the other hand, my particular individual contribution is unlikely to make any perceptible difference to the strength of the organization, just as adding one more hay stalk makes no difference to the height of a haystack; whereas, if the organization is successful, and achieves improvements in the safety standards of children's toys, I (or my children) will benefit whether I have joined the campaign or not. It is therefore rational for me to keep my money and my energy and look forward passively to the success of the campaign.

It will be noted that in order for this logic of non-participation to operate, the organization must be (a) a mass one, and (b) one seeking public ends, that is, ends which will be general in their application and not confined to those who have 'bought' them in some way. If the organization is very small, it might be rational to participate, despite the generality of its subsequent benefits, because in a small body every individual's contribution has an appreciable impact, so that if he or she stops making it the loss is immediately noticed. The public nature of the goal is important because, if I need to participate in order to achieve the ends, I cannot sit back and wait for this organization to deliver general benefits.

Trade-union membership may have similar characteristics: if it is a large union, my additional membership subscription will be such a tiny proportion of its assets that it will not affect the union's strength at all; on the other hand, if the union negotiates a wage increase or improvement in conditions, I shall gain whether or not I am a member. Therefore I act rationally to stay out of the union, keep my money and, possibly, avoid any opprobrium that union membership may attract from the employer. Nonmembership of unions may not, therefore, signify some kind of principled refusal to join; it may not even mean indifference towards them; it would simply, on this account, constitute a rational appraisal of the relationship between the cost of individual membership against the general nature of any gain, and the infinitesimal effect of my action on the union's strength.

Olson's account treats trade unions as one among many mass organizations. In doing so, it does not consider certain special problems resulting from the position of unions as representatives of the class of labour in the relationship between labour and capital. Two German sociologists have recently extended the analysis to tackle this point (Offe and Wiesenthal, 1980). First, they draw attention to the important fact that 'labour' consists of individual men and women, while 'capital' consists of units of money (pp. 73–4); units of capital can be added together, merged with each other, to provide single 'lumps' of capital, but workers, even when united, remain individual human beings with separate needs and wants. Capital is in that sense always a collectivity and automatically has the advantages of organization, while for workers organization presents special problems. A new, collective identity has to be forged out of the separate individual identities and imposed upon them (pp. 78–9). A further consequence of this is that it is much simpler for capitalists to work out what their rational interests are: namely, to maximize the return on their capital. Workers, in contrast, have not only to reach agreement on their varying individual human aims, but also have to accommodate these with the interests acquired in the collective identity which has made their organization possible (p. 96). This is an idea to which we shall return in later chapters. A simplicity of rational goals also makes it easier for capital to learn from experience:

This is because errors on the part of the capitalist are fed back to him from his market environment in unequivocal quantitative-monetary terms and within a relatively short time, whereas erroneous concepts of interest are not easily and rapidly detectable in the case of the worker. [*ibid*: 91]

For these reasons, not only is capital automatically a collectivity, but it is easier for various concentrations of capital (firms) to come together in organizations (trade associations, employers' associations) than it is for labour, because the organization simply has to process capital's fairly obvious interests (p. 85). In addition, of course, all except the smallest firms have less of a problem of being powerless units within a mass within their organizations than do workers. However, Offe and Wiesenthal possibly exaggerate capital's ease of organization; firms often show considerable resistance to any interference in their affairs, even from an association of other firms. It is notable that Offe and Wiesenthal have as their starting point German industry, which has always been used to a high level of organization, originating in its close relations with the state during industrialization under the Bismarck regime. Matters appear somewhat different from the perspective of British or American industry, with their long history of *laissez faire* and free competition (Shonfield, 1965).

On the basis of their analysis, Offe and Wiesenthal explore the means by which labour tries to solve its problems of organization, which lead it into new problems of bureaucratization and the division between leaders and members. We shall pursue this further in chapter 5. In the meantime their work is important in adding the crucial dimension of class inequality to the Olsonian analysis, while still remaining entirely within a framework of rational choice, or logic of action.

If the Olsonian account is correct, why does anyone join unions at all, apart from a handful of activists? This question may be answered partly in terms of the analysis itself, and partly in criticism of it. First – and this is what Olson himself does – we may look for means whereby some gains from the organization's activity are made dependent on membership. Second, we may look for means whereby the costs of membership are reduced, or, more accurately, the costs of membership relative to non-membership are reduced. Third, we may, rather critically of the original theory but nevertheless still within the framework suggested by it, examine the ways in which people may go about making a cost/benefit decision of this kind. Finally, we may query the extent to which trade-union membership does constitute a case of membership of a mass organization.

Selective benefits

Olson claims that a mass organization has to develop a range of services which are secondary, possibly even unrelated, to its central public purpose, but which meet some individual need of potential members and which are available only to members. These serve as selective incentives to membership. For a classic example we need look no further than the early trade-union movement. In addition to their work in pressing for improvements in wages and in working-class living standards, the early unions developed a range of individual services such as contributory funeral benefit schemes and insurance funds. These were important in recruiting members for immediate and tangible goals, while also affording the union funds and organizational facilities which could be used for more collective purposes. This explanation is intriguing because it suggests that, in order to recruit members, organizations may have to develop activities quite ancillary to their principal purpose.

There is a problem in the argument that should warn one against using it too freely: what constitutes an organization's *principal* purpose? Sometimes the individual benefit may have as much claim to be considered the primary goal of the organization as its collective activity. For example, the Consumers' Association in Britain lobbies governments over the improvement of law protecting the consumer, economic policies which it regards as being relevant to consumer interests and other matters which clearly count as collective goods in the Olsonian sense; that is, there is no connection between one's membership of the Association and one's capacity to benefit from any improvements which its work may secure. But the Association also publishes several journals, the most important being *Which?*, which advise readers on the qualities of products available in the shops, for use as a guide when making purchases. This is clearly a selective benefit; it is only possible to build up a collection of *Which?* by subscribing to it, and one immediately gains a personal benefit by being able to make a wise choice of products. One might therefore assume that *Which?* and the other journals were developed in order to provide an individual benefit to encourage people to join the Association and thereby help its mass campaigns. However, this is not so. Many people involved in the organization would regard the journals as the primary activity and the mass lobbying as a secondary, possibly even incidental, activity, and this thinking may well affect views within the Association as to the budgetary priority which the different activities are to enjoy.

Other cases may be more clear-cut; for example, several British trade unions organize discount arrangements for their members in certain shops. They do this as a minor attraction to membership in a strict Olsonian way, and no one could doubt that their primary purpose remains the collective one of pursuing improved wages and conditions for their members.

Interesting though this theme is, it is doubtful whether it constitutes a major explanation of trade-union membership in a country like Britain today, since union selective benefits are usually very small.[1] The main exception is the National Union of Agricultural Workers which maintains an unusually wide range of advisory services for its members, covering subjects normally dealt with by Citizens' Advice Bureaux and going far beyond anything to do with employment conditions. This can be explained partly in terms of the particular nature of agricultural labour, often in remote places far from such services as CABs and often involving workers of a low formal educational level who find it difficult to deal with the complexities of modern life. But Olsonian factors are also relevant. It is particularly difficult for farm workers to exercise collective strength because of the nature of their employment and its location in small scattered numbers; the collective goals are therefore particularly remote and this union does have a strong incentive to develop secondary benefits in a bid to drive up its membership figures.

Reducing the relative costs of membership

Olson's argument rests strongly on the assumption that membership of a voluntary body *costs* something – whether literal money-costs of subscription, cost in terms of time and effort, or costs in the sense of punishments imposed by opponents of the organization. Clearly, the higher these costs the bigger the problem of persuading people to participate in collective action. One should therefore expect to find collective organizations striving hard to reduce the costs of membership relative to those of non-membership. One way in which this is done by virtually all voluntary organizations is to reduce the demands made on the time and effort of members by establishing a permanent staff of paid officials. (This then gives rise to the new problem of leader-member relations which has loomed large in the literature on trade unions and which I shall consider in detail in chapter 5.) Reduction of financial cost is an obvious need, and there is considerable evidence that unions struggle hard to keep their subscriptions as low as possible, sometimes to the point of endangering their organizational capacity. They also try to make the extraction of the dues as automatic and as painless as possible by getting employers to agree to the 'check-off', that is, the deduction of union subscriptions at source, from the pay-packet, in the same way that income tax is collected.

I have used the cumbersome term 'reduce the costs of membership relative to those of non-membership', rather than talk simply of 'reducing the cost of membership', because a further strategy which unions, and sometimes other bodies, can pursue, is to increase the costs of non-membership. The most important means for doing this is for unions to insist on the closed shop or compulsory unionism (McCarthy, 1964; Gennard *et al.*, 1980). One could also regard the closed shop as being a kind of selective benefit as discussed above (Heath, 1976: 32): if you join the union you can have a job, if you are not a member you get no job. However, I think it is more readily understood as a means of increasing the costs of non-membership, since it counterbalances some of the techniques used by employers to increase the costs of membership.

The original closed shops were found in the old craft unions, where they continue and where they are sociologically very similar to the requirement to join a professional association imposed on members of the learned professions. One is allowed to seek employment as a member of a craft only if one possesses a union membership card, which is available only to those who have completed an apprenticeship. In this way the union limits employment in its trade to those who are qualified, ensuring a certain standard of skill and, more important to the union, limiting labour supply.[2] If only workers who have completed an apprenticeship can secure employment, the employer cannot try to drive down wages by seeking a wider pool of potential workers. Professional associations of medical practitioners, lawyers, engineers and other groups pursue a similar policy, with two exceptions. First, the professions have not limited their powers to allowing membership only to qualified persons; they have also controlled the training process itself, including maintaining an important say in the numbers which are trained. This gives these occupations a unique control over labour supply and goes a long way to explaining the high earnings traditionally associated with the professions. Second, historically, professionals have not been employees working for employers at all, but have been self-employed, working for fees paid directly by clients rather than for salaries. Over the years this sharp distinction has declined. The increasing size of organizations has led many legal and engineering practices, for example, to become large firms themselves, in which the partners employ other members of the profession as salary-earning employees. Large business corporations often employ their lawyers and engineers as direct employees, rather than engage them as consultants; and the same is true of national and local government. Further, the National Health Service has placed many medical practitioners in the position of employees. This important historical process has been accompanied, as one might expect, with a decline in the once clear distinction between trade unions and professional associations, and several associations now regard themselves as being, in part, unions.

This 'pre-entry' form of closed shop characteristic of the crafts and the professions is a model of ensuring union membership which is largely limited to occupations with a distinctive training process, such that an individual worker is going to regard himself as a member of a particular occupation whether he is in work or not. However, it is, rather paradoxically, also characteristic of certain occupations where employment is exceptionally insecure and temporary. One of the problems built into the Olson model is that, not only are the benefits to be expected from membership collective, but they are also spread out over time; you pay your subscription starting from the week you join, but it may be months before the union does anything for you, such as lodge a wage claim. This will be a particular disincentive for a worker whose job is likely to last only a few months. One therefore finds that many such occupations (for example, holiday catering) have particularly low levels of union membership. However, in some cases unions in such trades have, over the years, managed to convince at least some employers in an industry that there will be less trouble from the union if it is granted a pre-entry closed shop than if it is resisted. The two most important examples in Britain are shipping and acting. Dissimilar though those occupations and their practitioners may be, they have in common a pattern of work consisting of recruitment for a particular assignment (in the one case a voyage, in the other a film, play or show), followed by a spell of unemployment until the next assignment. The actors' union, Equity, and the National Union of Seamen have agreements with many employers that they will employ only workers who are members of these respective organizations. This radically transforms the individual actor's or seaman's calculations of whether or not it is worth his while joining a union.

Far more widespread than any of these cases of the pre-entry closed shop is the post-entry closed shop.[3] Under this arrangement there is no requirement that only union members may be recruited; instead, the employer accepts that, once a worker is engaged, he will be required to join a union (either a particular one, or one of a number represented in the plant) or he will be dismissed. Unions have won the agreement of employers to this in many industries, partly by threatening strikes or similar action, partly by offering co-operation on other matters in exchange, and partly because it may seem to offer the employer a guarantee of some kind of order. This last point needs to be explained. Managements are often able to reach agreements with union officials which are later rejected by groups of workers, who may want to take action to secure something better. Sometimes, though by no means always, the union will share management's disapproval of rejection of an agreement to which it has been party. It may then threaten sanctions against the workers who continue to agitate for a better agreement. If there is a closed shop in the firm, a threat of expulsion from the union would automatically mean dismissal from the firm of the worker concerned. The management could thereby achieve something which it dare not attempt itself: a threat of dismissal against workers who take strike or other action to improve their conditions. It must be stressed that this will not always occur (probably more common are cases of the closed shop being used as a sanction against workers who refuse to strike); but the possibility has sometimes been attractive to employers.

However achieved, the post-entry closed shop enables unions in ordinary semi-skilled occupations or those with no distinctive training periods to gain the advantage enjoyed by craft unions and many professional associations: the addition of the penalty of non-employment in the job or firm concerned to the costs of non-membership of the union.

This account of the closed shop is relevant to the frequent public debate over the issue. That debate is usually posed as one of freedom: should a worker not be free to join or not to join a union? Such a phrasing implies that the choice is then in some ways a balanced one, with the worker weighing up the benefits of joining against the disadvantages and costs. However, the theory of the logic of collective action suggests that an apparently free choice in fact contains a built-in bias against union membership. To take an example outside industrial relations, it is as though a government said: 'It is wrong that we force people to pay, through their taxes, for national defence. People should have a free choice as to whether or not to contribute to the defence budget. The armed forces will therefore be financed by voluntary contributions.' The result would be that many people would not make a defence contribution, not because they had a principled stand as pacifists, nor even because they thought defence was not worth having, but because they realized (i) that their individual contribution made only an infinitesimal difference to the total budget, while paying it made a big difference to their family budget, and (ii) that so long as some people were sufficiently concerned to ensure that the country had adequate defences, they would get the benefit, because the protection afforded by the armed forces in a modern society cannot be limited to some individuals in the society alone.

These arguments are relevant to the public debate about the closed shop; they reveal a certain naivety, or sleight of hand, in arguments against compulsory unionism based on a debate about 'freedom'. However, they cannot be taken as conclusive arguments in favour of the closed shop. First, it is, of course, still open for someone to object that unions are a bad thing and should not exist at all. Second and more subtly, one might argue that compulsion goes further than reducing the imbalance of the logic of collective action and creates too strong an imbalance the other way. Or, finally and rather differently, it can be argued that the closed shop prevents workers from showing their dissatisfaction with a union by leaving it, and therefore removes from union officials the penalty that might be expected to result from incompetence and inadequacy in serving their members' interests.

Government assistance, possibly through legal rights to union representation, is another means of reducing the costs of membership which unions in many countries have pursued, their political power (especially when parties close to them are in office) often being greater than their industrial strength against employers. It is interesting that for many years British unions did little to seek such assistance outside the public sector, preferring to fight for recognition themselves. This is probably explicable in terms of the exchange with the government which such a course would have required – assuming, that is, that governments would have been interested in such an exchange.[4] Government would have granted recognition rights on certain terms and conditions, probably designed to secure a particular structure to the union movement. British unions having, for various reasons, a great aversion to legal involvement in their affairs, preferred to struggle on without legal assistance in their battles for recognition, remaining free from any reciprocal obligations. In the early 1970s, however, most British unions abruptly changed their position,[5] and successfully lobbied for legal rights. In Acts of Parliament passed in 1974–6 they achieved considerable rights for workers to join and work actively for unions and to have these recognized by their employers.[6] This occurred at a time when the unions were feeling confident of having considerable political strength, and it is likely that they rated the cost of the exchange which government would impose on them rather low.

Making the cost-benefit decision

Rational-choice theories, like all economic theories, are not primarily interested in whether or not their assumptions about actors' motivations are empirically valid; so long as the observed behaviour fits that predicted by the theory, the theorist is content. For example, if the price of apples falls relative to that of pears, an economist will usually predict that the consumption of apples will increase and that of pears will decrease. He will not be very interested in the results of survey research on whether the consumers of fruit *think* their choice of individual types of fruit is affected by relative price or not; so long as their *behaviour* fits the prediction, he is confident that the motive assumed by his theory is useful.

This is often a reasonable position to adopt, if only because so often people are unaware of their own motives. Even if survey research reported that people said their choice between apples and pears was unaffected by relative price, the economist could still retort that, since their actual purchasing behaviour showed that consumption did vary with relative price, it has to be concluded that the survey respondents were not really aware of the motives of their own actions, and that he would go on preferring his account.

However, occasions arise when it is necessary to examine just how realistic the assumed motives are, because if they do in fact stray far from those anticipated in the theory, predictions based on the theory will go wildly wrong. This is sometimes the case in economics; it is even more of a problem with accounts of rational behaviour outside the central economic field where goods are being exchanged for known and quantifiable prices. It is important to investigate the reality of the rational exchange which we deem actors to make. To take our present example, how realistic is it to expect workers to make an assessment of the costs and benefits of joining a trade union, whether or not one builds into the calculation the particular problem of collective action?

When the parameters of choice over a particular course of action become too complex for us to make a proper assessment, and when information is either sparse or hard to achieve, we usually fall back on shorthand formulae, patterns of accepted beliefs, as hopefully containing distillations of wise calculation. The decision whether or not to join a union may often be of this kind. Among the possible gains will be: those advantages of collective action discussed at the beginning of the chapter – which may be discounted by the individual because of their collective character; the possibility that one may need the individual grievance-handling service that the union will provide for its members; avoidance of any opprobrium from fellow workers which may be directed against non-members. Among the costs will be: the financial contribution; and any opprobrium from management for being known as a union member. This may be a difficult calculation to make, the pattern of costs and benefits being largely a matter of trying to estimate what may happen in the future. Workers in such a situation may therefore fall back on perceptions about union membership or traditions of attitudes to unions which are available to them: are other members of their family union members, or are other members of their community? The more that this is so, the more is the person likely to regard union membership as normal. This is probably a major factor in the well-documented difference in levels of unionization among manual and non-manual workers. Most powerful will be the level of union membership in the person's own workplace. Quite apart from the issue of sanctions exerted against members or non-members in different contexts, the union density at the workplace might give some idea whether other workers there find membership worthwhile, and the worker may be willing to be guided by majority feeling, especially in occupations where workers have a high level of *esprit de corps* and mutual respect. In short, we would expect a worker starting work at a factory with 80 per cent union density to be more likely to join a union than if it were 50 per cent (Bain and Elsheikh, 1976: 67, 68, 85, 109).

Unions as 'non-mass' organizations

Crucial to the Olsonian theory of collective action is that the organization in question is so large that an individual member's contribution counts for nothing. At first sight most unions are such cases of 'mass' organizations, their membership running into hundreds of thousands. However, the reality of the union which the individual worker encounters is often a far more face-to-face group. There is considerable evidence from research that by 'the union' many workers mean the shop-floor organization rather than the remote national body with its headquarters in London. It is therefore quite probable that they encounter the union as a face-to-face group in which each person's contribution does make a relevant difference to the strength of the group. For example, Goldthorpe, Lockwood *et al.* (1968a: 106), discussing the fact that their samples of various types of manual workers took very little interest in the affairs of their union branch, but participated highly in shop-steward elections and other plant-level activity, comment:

> . . . it is evident that in the eyes of many of our semi-skilled workers, the unionism of the workplace is very largely *dissociated* from what they regard as the official activity of the unions to which they happen to belong. The former is what really matters – 'what concerns us' – while the latter they tend often to dismiss as having little at all to do with them.

In Olsonian terms, *if* workers had to orient themselves solely to the national organization, there would be a major problem of the logic of collective action. However they do not do so, but focus instead on the local face-to-face group. Or, as Goldthorpe and Lockwood put it:

> . . . such an orientation to trade unionism is one which 'makes sense' in terms of . . . the typical orientation of the workers in question towards their employment generally. That unionism should have little significance for them other than in relation to the immediate 'bread and butter' issues of their own work situation is entirely consistent with their definition of work as primarily a means to extrinsic ends: their main interest in the union, as in the firm, as that of the 'pay-off'. [*ibid*: 106]

Similar findings of the crucial importance of the local workplace as the focus of union identity are contained in more recent research (Batstone *et al.*, 1977), which goes on to answer the question which must obviously be raised: why, then, are workers organized in big national bodies, and not in plant-level unions on the Japanese pattern? The answer, say Batstone and his colleagues, lies in the role of the shop stewards. It is they who often turn to the services of the union for help and advice, and who need the legitimacy of its recognition in order to assert their own standing with management. The stewards, as it were, receive important selective benefits from the union which are crucial to their performance of the role of shop steward. They in turn therefore ensure that the men, who accredit *them* with legitimacy, retain their position as part of a wider union (*ibid*: 179–85).

This shop-level identification is most likely to occur where there is a good deal of plant-level activity. But even where the union organization is fairly centralized, the individual worker may encounter 'the union' as the face-to-face circle of workmates who constitute the union at his place of employment. This factor, coupled with the earlier point concerning the tendency to make short-cut decisions based on prevailing community customs when faced with complex choices, suggests that a local factory or office 'culture' may determine union membership. In that case unions do not suffer the worst problems of those mass organizations to which Olson's theory fully applies, that is, those which are recruiting within an anonymous mass population.

The rationality of variations in unionization

Collective-action theory is therefore of limited usefulness in explaining union membership. It does help pose the problem of union recruitment, and it continues to be a useful way of asking questions about how unions get members. But its own preferred explanation of how mass organization is possible – selective incentives – is not by itself adequate. As Barry argues (1970: 29), it is difficult to explain major differences in union membership across industries, countries or time periods in terms of different levels of selective incentives. Rather, indeed, the *primary* logic of collective action seems better equipped for this task. That is, union membership varies with the usefulness of the union to the workers in question. This 'usefulness' has two aspects. On the one hand, unionism will be more useful to a worker, the less able he is to use other means of advancing his interests – that is, the more *dependent* he is on collective action for improving his standard of living. For example, we would expect workers who have good chances of individual promotion to be less unionized than those who are treated by their employer as a mass. But following that logic alone, we should probably conclude that the poorer and more subordinate the workers, the more strongly unionized they will be, and that is far from being the case. We therefore have to take account of the other aspect of usefulness: the *ease* with which organization can be used. In many cases workers who might seem to have much to gain from organization will in practice have little opportunity to reap benefit.

These two different aspects of usefulness are orthogonally related, that is, they are quite independent dimensions. We may therefore plot them as two different axes, as shown in figure 2.1. Towards the top left-hand corner of the graph will be found those occupations who can use organization

Figure 2.1 Dimensions of usefulness of collective organization

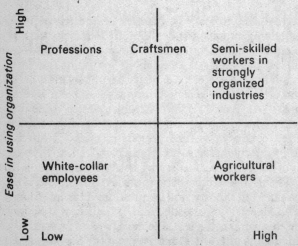

successfully, but who have a low level of dependence on it: for example, members of the professions who are powerful enough within the labour market because of the scarcity of their skills, but who also gain considerable advantages from joining a professional association. Skilled craftsmen are slightly less independent, but also enjoy considerable ease in using collective strength because of the closed nature of their unions. Towards the top right-hand side are those for whom organization is both easy and important, such as semi-skilled workers in plants where powerful shop-floor organizations have been very successful in gaining concessions from employers despite the relatively weak labour-market position of the workers. In the bottom left-hand corner are workers with particularly low levels of unionization, because organization is both difficult for them and not particularly important for their advancement. Examples here are white-collar workers, whose low level of unionism is better accounted for in these terms than by reference to class and status (as Bain, Coates and Ellis [1973] have shown). Their employers often refuse to recognize unions, and they can in any case rely on their work being individually evaluated and rewarded by the employer. Over time, increasing numbers of these workers are finding themselves in a 'mass' position, being regarded as one of many in a grade, and no longer being individually assessed by the employer (Lockwood, 1959; Braverman, 1974; Bain, 1970). At the same time, employer resistance to unions has been declining. On both counts, which both imply a shift towards the top right-hand corner, we would anticipate an increase in the level of unionization, and this has occurred. Whereas in 1948 only 33.8 per cent of male and 25.4 per cent of female white-collar workers were union members, by 1974 the proportions had risen to 44.5 per cent and 32.6 per cent respectively (Bain and Price, 1976).

Towards the bottom right-hand corner are those workers whose general position seems so weak that unionization ought to help them, but for whom organization is difficult. One example are agricultural workers, whose labour-market position is very weak indeed, but whose isolated working conditions make combination difficult (Newby, 1977).

It is possible to take some of the known sources of variation in unionization, and examine whether between them our two variables help explain them. For example, workers in large firms and plants have far higher levels of unionization than those in small firms and plants (Ingham, 1970). This is partly because workers are treated more like a mass, with both less scope for individual advancement and less fear of strike victimization, but partly because of the greater usefulness of the union on a large plant. As will be argued in a later chapter, the more that a company exists in a pure competitive market (a variable inversely related to size), the more difficulty it will have in raising prices because of increases in labour costs; and thus, the less can be achieved by union action in defiance of labour-market pressures. In contrast, a large firm, or a public monopoly, has a better though still finite chance of resisting market forces and will therefore be able to concede more to unions.

As another example, Clegg has shown (1976: ch. 2) that unionization varies between industries and indeed between countries according to the depth and extent of collective bargaining. Thus, only a small proportion of workers in France, where employers have strongly resisted collective bargaining and where the unions are not very interested in it either, join unions. Unionization is generally high in the public services, partly because governments have usually accepted unions; except in the USA, where public-sector unionism is weak and where until recent years governments rejected the idea of bargaining over public-service pay. In terms of our model, a union is clearly more useful to workers if collective bargaining is both widespread and concerned with important questions, rendering it easier to achieve success through combination.

Finally, women workers are almost universally more difficult to organize than their male counterparts. In some cases this might be attributed to greater difficulty in securing success through organization, where women are concentrated in such sectors as catering, characterized by temporary and casual employment. But the differential also holds true between men and women within the same occupation and working conditions. At first sight it is difficult to explain this in terms of less dependence on collective action, because in general women's labour-market position is weaker than that of men. However, there are grounds for arguing that women's dependence on unionism is less than men's because their general commitment to membership of the labour force is less. By commitment we do not here mean psychological attitude to work, but the extent to which the worker is dependent on paid employment for his or her long-term standard of living. Since union membership is intimately bound up with working life, the degree of dependence on unionism will be closely related to the degree of dependence on employment. For many female workers, paid employment has been a temporary condition until marriage or the birth of a child. Even for those not in that category, married women's wages have often been regarded as a second income in the family, after the husband's, to be used for less 'essential' purchases. Similar arguments concerning commitment to the labour force apply to migrant workers and immigrants, who often combine work in modern industry with seasonal returns to their region or country of origin to work on the land (Castles and Kossack, 1973). Even after the reality of seasonal return has ended, belief in it may still condition workers' attitudes to industrial employment for a while. As we would expect, migrants and immigrants usually have lower levels of union membership than fully industrialized workers.

Further evidence of the lower commitment of women to membership of the labour force can be seen in their lower tendency to register as unemployed and claim unemployment benefit when they lose their jobs. Published statistics regularly report higher proportions of the male than of the female section of the workforce as unemployed, though we know from other evidence that women are in fact far more likely to be made unemployed during periods of slack demand than are men. The reason for the discrepancy is that most women have not regarded themselves as long-term potential employees.

In recent years this differential has declined, which is evidence of increasing commitment to long-term labour-force participation by women. This tallies with what one knows from other sociological evidence of a change in women's attitudes to themselves and their place in society, revealed statistically in such indicators as the number of married women and mothers remaining in work (Wainwright, 1978). If this is so, we should expect a rise in female union membership, and this is indeed the case. In 1948 only 25.7 per cent of women workers were union members, against 52.9 per cent of men. By 1974 the female proportion had risen to 36.7 per cent, against 56.9 per cent for men (Bain and Price, 1976).

There is therefore considerable evidence of rationality in the pattern of union membership, in the sense that membership tends to be higher among workers for whom unions can make relatively important achievements. Workers who can achieve their goals primarily through individual means, or who are less likely to regard the role as worker as a significant part of their lives, or for whom unions are unlikely to be able to do much, are less likely to be in membership. In addition to examining these cross-sectional differences, contrasting different types of worker, we can see a similar responsiveness to varying economic circumstances *over time*. This also implies rational calculation.

Bain and Elsheikh (1976) explain variations in the rate and direction of union-membership growth primarily in terms of four variables: rates of change in prices, rates of change in money-wages, the level and/or rate of change of unemployment, and the level of union density. The last of these is largely structural and statistical in its effect, and the third (unemployment) partly reflects the fact that it is simply difficult to recruit or retain union membership among the unemployed. But the first two factors, and to a certain extent the third, imply calculation. When prices are rising, workers (i) feel that their standard of living is being threatened and turn to a union to help them raise wages, and (ii) realize that, in buoyant markets, their employer will be able to concede wage rises which he can pass on in the general context of rising prices. Rising money-wages lead workers to conclude that the chances are good for pressing further gains; they are made confident that they can risk collective action. Finally, unemployment inhibits membership because there is less that unions can achieve during a recession; there is less scope for wage rises, and employers are better able to victimize activists and replace strikers by other workers.

Bain and Elsheikh's work is based on long historical time series. In very recent years it has been notable how, in several countries, union membership has continued to rise despite rising unemployment – in the UK not declining until 1980, despite unemployment levels throughout the 1970s that were higher than those of the 1950s and 1960s. The answer probably lies in the fact that during the 1970s unions acquired many new rights to negotiate redundancy terms and the timing of closures. Workers may now see unions as capable of protecting them from the implications of unemployment, which was not the case in previous periods of high unemployment.

All the arguments in this chapter on the reasons why different types of worker may or may not unionize show that we are here dealing with a complex choice, affected by several variables. Some points seem clear, such as the rise in female unionization caused by increasing labour-force commitment. But many of the variables may be working against each other. For example, we would predict a very low level of union membership in acting and shipping on the basis of reasoning about the impact of temporariness on a worker's decision whether or not to join a union; until we learn that the unions here have been able to adjust the cost-benefit calculation by a partly successful closed shop. We would predict high levels of unionization in all large companies; until we learn of the vigorous punishment of union members carried out by some giant American corporations. What we really need is evidence of unionization levels across a large number and a wide range of work situations. We could then construct a lengthy equation in which all the potential explanations of different membership levels are included, and proceed to test them. This would reveal which explanations are the most powerful and which, if any, are redundant or unhelpful. In the absence of such a test we can only draw attention to potential explanations, hint at some examples, and remain silent about their relative impact.

3 The Means of
   Collective Action

Having established a rationale for combination, we have to determine how that combination expresses its power against the employer. The most obvious answer provides a good starting point: the strike or withdrawal of labour. While striking occupies only a minute proportion of the time and energy of most unions, nearly all the other means through which combinations of workers exercise power and influence depend in the last analysis on the threat, or even just the possibility of a threat, to withdraw labour.

Unlike serfs and slaves, wage labourers and salaried employees can individually leave a job whenever they like, subject to serving a fairly short period of notice. There have been exceptions: indentured apprentices had few rights to leave their employer; members of the armed forces are usually bound to service contracts lasting several years; and foreign workers in certain countries sometimes have their permission to stay in the country linked to their employment in a particular firm. It is notable that treatment by superiors of workers in such a position is usually worse than that of those who can leave. In general, the liberty individually to leave a particular employment is a feature of the capitalist economy which, given certain conditions, provides some kind of guarantee of good treatment. *If* a worker can easily go elsewhere to find better conditions, employers who want to retain their workers have to ensure that they provide acceptable conditions in the first place. However, if there are few alternative jobs to which the worker can go, that freedom is of little use; when there is high unemployment and virtually no social provision for the unemployed, as was often the case during early capitalism, it may be merely the freedom to starve.

The power *collectively* to leave employment, which we understand by the strike, goes far further than this individual right in asserting employees' power. By leaving *en masse*, the workers' aim is to bring all work in the section, company or industry concerned to a halt. Whereas the individual worker who leaves is fairly easily replaced from the labour market, it is far more difficult to replace an entire workforce – and anyway, as we shall see, the union usually takes more active steps to ensure that no new workers are engaged to replace those striking. The strikers, again unlike the individual worker leaving his job, intend to return to their jobs once their demands have been met; they are not leaving their employment, and are therefore not immediately dependent on the availability of other work.

Against these advantages over the individual leaving his job, strikers are weak in that, temporarily losing their work, they lose their means of support. And, unless the union can do something to prevent it, the employer may dismiss strikers and engage new labour.

These points go to the heart of the weakness of the union's position in a confrontation with the employer. On the face of it, the strike is a powerful weapon; in an industrial society workers, especially manual workers, are the most immediately indispensable class. If they all stop work, the society comes to a complete halt. In recent times the French strikes of May 1968, the British coal-mining strike of winter 1973–4 and the British road-haulage and public-service strikes of winter 1978–9 have all shown that power. In the latter nineteenth century, particularly in France, considerable weight was placed on the possibility of a general strike of all workers which would bring existing society to its knees and force revolutionary social changes. But it never happened. The reason is the great weakness of labour in its relations with capital, which no amount of organization can fully offset. Except in most unusual cases, capital can change its form, go away, move to sectors or countries where it can be more profitably employed; labour can do none of these things so quickly. It comprises individual human beings, who have a constant need for subsistence, and who can move large geographical distances in search of alternative employment only with great risk and difficulty (Hyman, 1975: 17–25 and ch. 4; Offe and Wiesenthal, 1980). As Blau has pointed out (1964), in any exchange (including that of the labour contract), the party which has the greater range of alternatives to the exchange in question has far greater power to dictate its terms.

Labour consumes most of its income shortly after receipt, in order to subsist and maintain a few creature comforts. In the first stages of a prolonged strike, workers have to reduce their consumption standards. If the strike continues, they are forced to use up their savings and perhaps sell consumer durables or relinquish goods being bought on hire purchase. After that they are without resources. The position of capital is quite different. The earnings from capital are not providing subsistence for anyone making decisions on its behalf.[1] Further, while in the short and medium term plant and equipment are fixed, capital which is held in the form of liquid assets can be moved around the world in search of profitable outlets; it cannot be blocked by workers on strike. In general, therefore, the longer the strike the weaker the workers' position. For the workers to gain a victory in a strike the employers have to need a quick settlement, as is often the case. At the moment a strike is called, neither side has lost anything. As time goes by they both lose more and more, and eventually both capital and labour could reach the point of ruin. But the important point is that the workers' position declines far more rapidly. Relatively quickly they could, in the absence of external means of help, reach the point of desperation, where they have almost nothing left to lose but life itself. Figure 3.1 traces the way in which resources might be expected to deteriorate during the course of a long strike. It shows the slower rate of deterioration of capital's resources, and how

Figure 3.1 Deterioration of resources during a strike

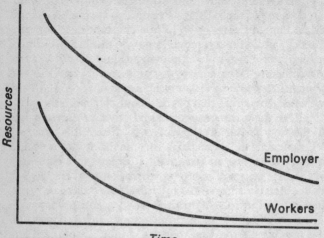

labour's losses must eventually stabilize at a level very slightly above zero. (This is because when labour has 'nothing left to lose' it obviously cannot go on losing more.) Eventually the workers in a desperate strike will make the calculation that surrender is inevitable, and that the cost will never be made good. This decision is likely to be made by different workers at different times, and there will be a gradual troop back to work. This is because the decision is based on inadequate information about how likely is a concession (on which workers will hold varied opinions), and on different evaluations of loss against desperate need.[2]

If employers are in such a superior position to the workers, why do not all strikes last a long time until workers are driven to desperation? Why do employers ever make concessions if their staying power is superior? To understand this we must evaluate the position from the point of view of an employer facing a strike. He knows the workers are losing at a faster rate than he is, but he is still losing; this loss has to be set against the cost of a concession which

Figure 3.2 Resistance curves during industrial disputes

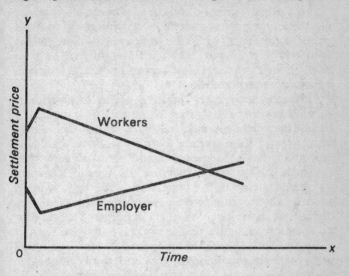

will end the strike. For example, if a strike of just a few days for a pay claim worth £5 million will lose an order worth £100 million, the employer will probably consider it worthwhile to concede. Decisions are usually not this clear, but in general the longer the strike the bigger the loss, both absolutely and relative to the cost of concessions.

If, therefore, the employer becomes convinced of the workers' ability to prolong a strike, he will be prepared to make a bigger concession to end it than he was at the outset. At the same time the gain workers are seeking will diminish with time as their capacity for resistance runs down. In other words, if we plot changes over time in the price at which the workers and the employers will be willing to reach agreement, as in figure 3.2, we should be able to predict the point at which a compromise will be reached to end the strike. On the y axis we plot the wage at which either side will settle the strike, and on the x axis we plot the duration of the strike. At time 0, the beginning of the strike, the positions of the two sides (which represent the workers' original demand and the employer's offer) are far apart. As time passes, the employer is prepared to make greater concessions, while the workers are willing to take a smaller rise in order to get back to full earnings. The point at which their two curves intersect will be that at which an agreement is finally made.

Although the workers' position begins to deteriorate immediately, in that they start to lose wages, we should not assume that they are immediately likely to drop their settlement price. Before starting a strike, workers should be expected to have made an estimate as to how long they anticipate it to last; within that period we should not expect their resistance to drop. In fact, during the early days of a strike we should anticipate the *opposite* pattern; the bigger their demand, the longer they will be prepared to strike for it. Therefore, in figure 3.2 the workers' curve is shown as *rising* at first; it is once the strike lasts beyond that initial period of their expectations that the settlement curve begins to drop downwards. Similarly, the employer should be expected to make forecasts of the likely course of a dispute and, again, during the period covered by that estimate, he will be prepared to make a longer stand the bigger the demand. In this section we consider the cases of strikes in which agreements are made beyond the period expected by either side; that is, during the period of declining resistance by both sides. However, in heavily institutionalized bargaining systems, as discussed in a later section of this chapter, it is possible for strikes to end much earlier than this. The likely pattern of strikes terminated during the early 'upward' parts of both sides' curves will be considered in the following chapter.

Of course, a simple diagram like 3.2 does not take us far; we cannot tell *a priori* the precise shape of the curves. However, it raises some interesting questions about strike behaviour. For example, if there is an intersection point at some moment in the strike where agreement will be reached, why cannot unions and employers predict this in

advance and so avoid the strike altogether? Part of the
answer is that they often do precisely this; there are many,
many instances of disputes which never reach the strike
stage, and one of the reasons is often that experienced
negotiators on both sides assess in advance the breaking
point of their adversary, and make an early move to compromise at that level. But there will be cases where that is
not possible, when neither side can estimate the other's
position accurately. Unions may not know enough about
the market position of an employer to be able to tell just
how much he can afford to concede; employers may not be
able accurately to assess the strength of workers' solidarity.
A recent study of the organization of strikes (Batstone *et al.*,
1978; chs. 12, 13) brings out very clearly the importance of
the problem for strike organizers of guessing how likely the
employer is to make a concession. Matters are not made any
easier by the fact that both sides will usually be deliberately
trying to give a false impression of their position to the
other. Management, for example, may well claim that a
strike will lead to mass redundancy, or to bankruptcy, well
before such a situation is in fact being faced. The workers
have to decide whether or not to call the management's
bluff, and this involves yet another difficult decision based
on inadequate information. In 1980 and 1981 a number of
disputes at BL Cars ended following extraordinary threats
of plant closures and disciplinary action by the management. As recently as two or three years previously, workers
at BL would probably have called the management's bluff
and continued with their strike; but within a context of
sharply rising unemployment and repeated government
threats to cut off subsidies to the firm, fewer workers have
been willing to take that risk.

The difficulties facing unions in particular when trying
to estimate the respective strengths of the two sides is
further illustrated by Batstone *et al.* (*ibid*: 172) when they
point out that shop stewards may have difficulty estima-
ting the capacity of their *own members* to endure a long
strike:

In part, the very development of a normative group atmosphere in favour of a strike made it more difficult to assess individuals' feelings because many members were aware of the informal verbal sanctions for going against the norm. But this atmosphere also existed at the mass meeting, and it was something developed by the stewards.

In general, this mutual ignorance can be expected to be greatest when both sides have little experience of dealing with each other, or when major changes in the economic or organizational environment render it difficult to make predictions about future behaviour on the basis of past experience. Thus, strikes among groups of workers new to industrial action are often long and bitter, and most examples of strikes as 'fights to the finish' are caused by employers refusing to allow union membership among their employees (Hyman, 1972: 19).

A further question raised by figure 3.2 concerns what happens after the intersection point of the two curves. The figure suggests the paradoxical possibility that, as time passes, the employer would be willing to offer more than the workers demand! To consider this situation we need some more complex understanding of the employer's position than this simple figure gives us. We must take account of the fact that a strike for a wage demand may have two effects on an employer. First, he may calculate that if he pays wages above a certain level he will lose business and possibly go bankrupt. There will therefore be a point in bargaining beyond which the employer, correctly or not, is convinced he dare not go. (This point will rarely be announced to the workers at the start of the conflict; the employer will bluff, pretending that he faces bankruptcy at a much earlier point, hoping to make a deal at a level of pay considerably below his true marginal rate.) This means that at a certain point the employer's curve in 3.2 is likely to become a horizontal line: no matter how long the strike continues, he will make no higher offer, as he believes that to do so will bankrupt the business. However, he is also subject to a second logic: eventually, the strike itself will

Figure 3.3 Possible conflict outcomes with various workers' resistance curves

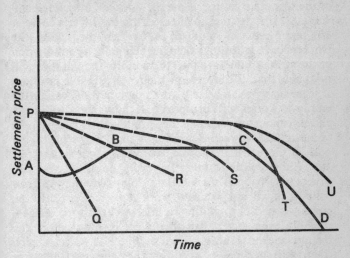

lose him so many orders that he decides the business is permanently impaired. He may decide to close the business, go bankrupt, take back labour only at very low rates of pay, or offer higher pay but to a much reduced workforce. In other words, his curve will dip *downwards*; as time passes and the strike continues, he offers decreasing levels of pay, reaching zero at the point of business closure.

An employer's curve is therefore probably shaped as in line ABCD in figure 3.3, though again the precise dimensions will be dependent on economic and social circumstances. At first (AB) the employer is willing to offer increasing concessions to get work restarted, until at B he reaches his 'sticking point', the highest level of pay which he believes he dare offer while remaining in business. He stays at this level, despite the continuation of the strike, until point C. At this point the strike begins to do what he regards as irreparable damage to the business; his willingness to offer wage increases declines until, at D, the firm goes into liquidation. Now, the relative position to this curve of the workers' curve is clearly crucial to the outcome of the dispute. Let us assume the workers' initial demand was at P. If it declines to intersect the employer's curve at any point between A and B, as, for example, in PQ, the workers have failed to maximize their gain; a continuation of the strike could have won them more, though they will not know that. PR represents their best possible position; it intersects precisely at B, the point beyond which the employer's offer will not increase. If the workers' militancy and resistance are such that they prolong the strike to some point in time between B and C, say to S, they will still get nothing more than they could have had by ending the strike at R. If they continue the strike beyond point C, one of two things may happen. At a certain point they may suffer a collapse of will and return to work at a rate lower than the employer had been willing to offer earlier in the strike – possibly even lower than they were earning before the dispute started. This is shown by line PT. Alternatively, their resistance may be such that they continue the strike beyond the point where the employer closes the business, as in PU. These strikers will never be re-engaged by their original employer.

Of course, the workers' resistance curve may have a shape which is the mirror image of that of the employer; after a 'flat' period where they rest at an irreducible minimum demand, they may say they actually need higher pay than they were seeking before, in order to compensate them for their losses during the strike. The problem is that by then the firm is likely to have disappeared. The workers' equivalent to the employer's tactic of firm-closure is, of course, to seek work elsewhere, and this often happens during prolonged disputes. However, given that long strikes usually take place during recessions, when employers are not confident that demand will remain high if their labour costs rise, that search for alternative work will be difficult. Nevertheless, it remains the case that if a strike does not end in a settlement, it ends with a severing of the employment relationship through either closure of the firm or the workers' leaving employment. At this point we should recall the arguments of Offe and Wiesenthal, discussed in the previous chapter, concerning the intrinsic weakness of labour in its relations with capital. Not only is it easier for capital to 'go away', in view of its greater ease of mobility; but from the point of view of the *union*, the disintegration of a workforce after a long strike means that the organization which it had built up is destroyed. Individual workers who leave the firm in dispute may find satisfactory jobs elsewhere, but for the organization it is a total defeat.

It is central to the understanding of a prolonged dispute to realize that neither workers nor employer will have precise knowledge of the respective curves of their opponents; indeed, they will not know very much about their own curves, especially on the union side where there is so much dependence on the loyalty of individual workers. Both sides will try to find out what they can about each other, but at the same time they will both be trying to give each other misleading information, bluffing and trying to call the other's bluff. Thus, workers may have a good idea that the employer has a resistance curve something like that shown in 3.3, but they will have only a poor idea whether a move by them to reach an agreement will be striking that curve at, say, PQ, PS or even PT. All this helps explain why, after the conclusion of a long strike, there are often bitter recriminations between the union representatives who signed the agreement and militant workers who claim that, if only the strike could have lasted a little longer, far bigger concessions could have been won; in other words, they will insist that an agreement has been reached on PQ rather than PR. Other workers may argue that the union could have gained the eventual agreement earlier if only it had been prepared to come to reason (i.e., an agreement has been made at PS).[3] Marxists, whether as union activists or as academic and political observers, are in a special position in that, at whatever point an agreement is reached, they always argue that it is a sell-out. This is not because they always judge agreements to have been at PQ, but because they reject some of the major assumptions behind the whole argument of this chapter. As can be appreciated by looking at figures 3.2 and 3.3, while I have assumed a conflict between capital and labour, I also assume a shared interest; both capital and labour are seen as losers if a lengthy strike destroys a business. For Marxists the position is quite different; the workers' best long-term interests lie precisely in the destruction of businesses, though different schools of Marxists disagree on the part to be played in that destruction by strikes and wage demands. Glyn and Sutcliffe (1972), whose arguments were discussed in chapter 1, are Marxists who do give wage demands such a role. For them, therefore, the prolongation of conflict up to and beyond the point of business liquidation must always be in the workers' long-term interests, even if in the short term it may mean unemployment, for only through the collapse of capitalism can workers bring about a new mode of production in which they are not at all dependent on employment relationships. We shall return to this issue in the next chapter.

In modern industrial relations, strikes of the desperate kind depicted in figure 3.3 seem very remote; various institutions of mediation and compromise usually get to work before such a position is reached within an *individual* strike. However, something very similar may happen in firms or industries subject to repeated small conflicts over a period of years. Each individual dispute may be concluded rapidly, or, indeed, agreements may be reached without a strike at all; but gradually the company moves closer to bankruptcy, or at least major redundancies, as a result of rising wage costs. At a certain point the workers find the employer's resistance suddenly far stiffer than that to which they have become accustomed to finding.

Strategies for increasing organized strength

The problem of the curve beyond the intersection in figure 3.2 will influence union and employer strategies. Workers and unions will be trying constantly to improve workers' capacity to resist, to enable them to raise the position of their curve so that they can strike for longer and intersect the employer's curve at a higher wage level; and to shorten the employer's capacity to resist. Employers will be trying to force the workers' curve down or to improve their own capacity to resist. In exploring some of the means which unions will use to try to improve the relative position of their curve, we shall be able to explain several characteristic union policies. (The same could, of course, be done for employers, but the centre of our focus here is the union.)

Timing of strikes
Since capital's capacity to withstand a strike declines more slowly than labour's, labour has a good deal to gain from a strike timed to catch an employer at a point where he will need a quick solution (Batstone *et al.*, 1978: 30–1). Some industries are peculiarly vulnerable in this way. One of the most prominent is the newspaper industry, where the product is uniquely perishable. Nobody wants to buy yesterday's daily newspaper, so if a particular edition does not appear on the newsstands at the appropriate time it is lost. A threatened strike by workers printing a daily paper therefore usually evokes an immediate response by the employers. When the management of *The Times* newspaper embarked on a lock-out of its printing staff which lasted from December 1978 to November 1979, it was a calculated risk that the enormous losses sustained would enable a breakthrough in an agreement on new manning arrangements that would eventually save the company money. But it is rare that newspaper-owners make such a calculation. Similar examples of the power of sudden strikes are those of exhibition contractors on the eve of major exhibitions

which will be unable to open unless they complete their work on time. Somewhat more generally, employers in industries with long production lines, such as the motor industry, are likely to want a speedy settlement to a strike. If the flow of a production line is impeded by a dispute among a small number of men, the output of an entire factory can be affected. Large multi-national firms have developed a way round this problem by ensuring that they are never dependent on the production line in one country for the supply of a particular product; they have developed 'multiple sourcing', that is, the production of identical products in more than one country, so that in the event of a strike affecting the production line in country A, production is stepped up in country B. So long as unions find it difficult to combine their actions internationally, they will be unable to combat this.

The effect of the timing of strikes on the relative power of management and unions is not limited to types of product or production; also relevant is the state of the product market. Clearly, an employer with full order-books, struggling to meet commitments to customers, will be more willing to make concessions to labour to ensure that production continues than will an employer facing falling demand. Indeed, an employer in the latter case may actually *welcome* a strike because it saves him the need either to pay workers whose products are not being purchased or to make workers redundant and incur the costs of redundancy payments:

> One can readily imagine that a management which has reached the limits of its ability to stock finished cars or persuade its dealers to take more, and is afraid that sufficient short-time will be difficult to organize but that lay-offs will result – if not in official strikes or public criticism – in a labour shortage when trade recovers, may accept an unofficial dispute as a heaven-sent occasion to suspend production temporarily. [Turner *et al.*, 1967: 118]

Periods of economic expansion and high demand are usually accompanied by short, opportunistic strikes, and periods of recession by fewer, long, desperate strikes. An important recent example of the latter was that in the British state steel industry in early 1980. The strike, over a wage increase, was the first complete strike of the industry for many years, lasted twelve weeks and took place against a background of over-capacity in the steel industry, which was making massive losses. As the government was quick to point out, since the industry was making losses, there was probably a saving in not having to pay workers' wages for the duration of the strike.

Reducing the cost of strikes

So far we have assumed that during a strike workers, deprived of their wages, are without income. This is clearly a major source of their weakness, of the sharply declining shape of their resistance curve over time in the simple case. It is not surprising that unions have tried to do something about this. The most obvious measure they can take is to establish strike funds by setting aside a portion of their subscription income. These funds can then be used to make payments to workers on strike in lieu of their wages. How much can be achieved in this way is limited by the willingness of members to pay subscriptions; if the subscription becomes very high, workers will decide not to join the union. For example, French unions seem to find membership recruitment very difficult. As a result, union subscriptions are kept very low and there is no possibility of paying strike pay. It is therefore not surprising to learn that French strikes are characteristically very short, usually demonstrations rather than strikes. In Germany, in contrast, where workers seem willing to pay very large subscriptions for union membership, there is a tradition of very high strike pay; a German worker on strike will expect to receive at least 80 per cent of his usual income in strike pay (Clegg, 1976: 78–9).

The relationship of cause and effect in these variables is not obvious. The tradition of short demonstration-strikes in France is partly explained by the fact that, on the one hand, employers have refused to bargain with unions, while on the other hand so many economic decisions in France are made by government that it makes sense for the unions to address many of their demands to it rather than to employers (Shorter and Tilly, 1974). The short, large-scale demonstration-strike designed to embarrass and attract the attention of government is therefore understandable in the French context. The German pattern of large strikes during the course of which workers will need to be financially helped can also be explained in terms of that country's industrial-relations history. In Germany, and also in the Scandinavian countries, unions and employers alike are very centrally organized (Clegg, 1976; Jackson and Sisson, 1976; Streeck, 1980). Employers will join together to resist a strike, being unwilling to break rank or to take advantage of each other's industrial problems; indeed, individual employers who go against an agreed policy may be fined by their employers' association. They are therefore likely to meet a strike by solid resistance, probably locking out workers who have not been called out on strike. When a conflict occurs it is likely to be a long drawn-out affair. Given what we know about the increasing relative weakness over time of the workers' side in a conflict, this willingness of employers to take a strike in solidarity would leave the union very weak. The establishment of large strike funds by German unions, and the high levels of strike pay which they provide, can therefore be seen as a response to this; the workers, too, are prepared for long strikes. The implication of all this is that both sides in German and Scandinavian industry are ready for particularly long resistance curves; and this in turn may help explain why, given the enormous cost to both sides of prolonged strikes, employers and unions alike in those countries try very hard to avoid open conflict.[4]

British unions have far larger funds than the French, but small compared with the Germans'. It is interesting that the strike strategies of British industrial relations can also be seen as lying between those of these two countries. The

'French' short demonstration-strike is almost non-existent in Britain; like German strikes, British strikes nearly always concern relations between workers and employers, not unions and the government, and their aim is a bargaining outcome, not a political gesture. There is therefore greater need than in France for a capacity to make a strike last. However, the pattern of solidary employers facing centrally organized unions, familiar in Germany and Scandinavia, is not the normal case here. Conflicts are typically short, restricted in size and scope, with both sides trying to move to an early resolution.

However, that pattern is not universal; it applies more to some industries than to others and has been becoming less true in recent years. Many important strikes have been in the public sector, where the government has increasingly adopted a position of resistance; while in the private sector the growing weakness of the British economy has led many employers to prefer to endure a long strike in order to reduce relative wage costs than to compromise for an easy if expensive resumption of production – especially since falling demand reduces the amount of orders likely to be lost during a strike. How have workers managed to finance these strikes if union strike pay is low, or in some cases non-existent? For example, during the great coal-mining strike of 1974 the National Union of Mineworkers paid out *no strike pay at all*.

One answer may be that strikers have relied on social security benefits. A striker is not permitted to draw social security benefit himself, but his wife is allowed benefit for herself and her children. It is therefore not at all surprising that employers, seeking always to weaken the workers' strike resistance, should have pressed hard for the abolition or limitation of the right of strikers' families to claim social security benefit, and that the present Conservative government, responsive to employers' interests, should have met this demand. Since 1980, social security offices have *assumed* that wives and children of strikers are receiving strike pay of a certain specified amount from the union, and pay any benefit due only beyond that amount. The onus is then shifted to the union to provide strike pay. For many unions this may mean either a large financial cost or an increase in subscriptions which may lead to a loss of membership; in either case, unions would be weakened.

However, there is some dispute as to the extent to which strikers do rely on social security benefits for their families to finance strikes. The recent political interest in the issue has led to research into the matter (Durcan and McCarthy, 1974). As Clegg (1979: 281) points out, supplementary benefit is not payable until a strike has lasted two weeks and, since 80 per cent of strikes last for less than that, it is in only 20 per cent of cases that there could be any effect. Research on some prolonged strikes (Clegg, 1979: 281–4; Cole, 1975; Gennard and Lasko, 1975) has suggested that, while there is some recourse to supplementary benefit and also to tax rebates, strikers' own savings are the main source of strike finance. The importance of union strike pay varies considerably from union to union, but is not often large; it is estimated that strike pay rarely constitutes more than 10 per cent of normal earnings (Gennard, 1977).

A notable feature of this issue is the importance to it of the expected length of strikes. During the 1950s and 1960s the typical British strike was short and small in scale; employers complained of this very fact, arguing that a number of unpredictable short strikes was more disruptive than single, long, large ones such as are characteristic of North American disputes. During short strikes the issue of financial support does not arise, because the dispute does not last long enough for the workers to feel the impact of the lost wages. The current interest in financial support by employer-interests may be a sign that employers anticipate that the recent tendency for strikes to last longer will continue.

Financial support for strikes raises another important question: the centralization of decision-making within unions. This question *per se* is the subject of chapter 5, but some attention must be paid to it here. Strike funds are almost always controlled centrally; it is usually only at that level that it is possible to aggregate enough small contributions from members to be able to make sizeable pay-outs to groups of strikers. Clearly, those responsible for the strike fund, the union leadership, cannot allow groups of strikers all over the country to make claims on the strike fund whenever they call a strike, or the fund would be out of control. Strike pay is therefore only possible for strikes authorized by the union leadership, that is, official strikes. The more the industrial-relations system requires dependence on union strike pay, the more are decisions about strike action likely to rest with the union leadership (Clegg, 1976: 78); in other words, the more centralized will the union movement be – though some unions seem relatively content to recognize a strike and allocate strike pay retrospectively (Clegg, 1979: 281 ff).

Increasing strike effectiveness
So far we have assumed that all the workers in a plant or industry strike voluntarily and that, if they strike, the employer has no alternative but to close the plant and await their return. But both of these assumptions may be incorrect. There may be only limited support for a strike; this should not surprise us, since we have seen how striking can impose considerable sacrifices on the workers concerned. A strike that is not fully supported will be less effective, since some work will continue, lengthening the employer's resistance and thereby strengthening his position. If only a minority of workers strikes, the employer may be able to discipline or dismiss them; indeed, in some circumstances an entire striking workforce may be sacked and replaced by non-strikers.

Batstone *et al.* (1978: 28, 29) describe this issue as that of the 'substitutability' of strikers. Different workers vary considerably in their degree of substitutability. One source of variation will be skill; clearly it is far harder to find sudden replacements for highly trained craftsmen than for unskilled labourers, which is one reason why craft unions have guarded their traditions so jealously. A different kind of variation, and one on which we concentrate here, concerns the varying willingness of other workers to take on the jobs of strikers. One of the central aims of union organization is to ensure solidarity among workers so that they will refuse to do the work of striking colleagues, though even a union may suspend this very strong presumption in cases of unofficial strikes by small numbers of workers which put large numbers of union members out of work.

Much trade-union history is the history of attempts to reduce the substitutability of striking workers. These have not always been successful; there are many examples from the nineteenth century of English strikers being dismissed and replaced by Irishmen, brought over from their own impoverished country for the purpose. Cases of strikes being weakened or rendered impossible by lack of support are still commonplace. Unions' main response has been to develop their own disciplinary sanctions over non-strikers, so that the individual worker deciding whether or not to strike has to weigh in the balance the punishment he will receive from his union for not striking against any punishments, together with loss of income, the employer will impose for striking. Where a bitter struggle is in progress between company and union, this can impose some very cruel dilemmas on individual workers.

Barry (1970: 44), considering the organization of a strike as a difficult case of the logic of collective action, describes these sanctions as instances, in Olsonian terms, of selective negative incentives. He goes on to point out that most of these sanctions depend on moral or physical pressures at the community level, and that therefore the best hope for an employer trying to break a strike despite the existence of such sanctions lies in recruiting complete outsiders, preferably foreigners speaking a different language, from beyond the local community and not vulnerable to its sanctions. No doubt he had in mind the case of Irish workers in nineteenth-century England referred to above. Such actions by employers have sometimes led organized workers

and their leaders to adopt hostile attitudes towards outsiders and racial minorities. Engels, for example, had an
almost racist attitude towards the Irish (Baudouin *et al.*,
1978), and for many years Australian unions insisted
on a 'white Australia' policy, opposing Chinese immigra-
tion.

But what sanctions can a trade union wield which can
compare with the employer's ability to deprive a man of his
entire livelihood? In the nineteenth century, when the employer's power to dismiss might mean the difference
between subsistence and starvation, this was a problem
indeed. It is perhaps not surprising that there were many
cases of threatened, and sometimes actual, violence against
workers who refused to join a strike. The achievement of
the closed shop, discussed in chapter 2, eased the problem,
initially for the craft workers, but gradually for others as
well. Once a closed shop has been established, the threat of
expulsion from the union can be used as a sanction, and
acquires the same force as the employer's threat of dismissal. Where the closed shop does not apply, or where the
sanction of expulsion cannot be used (for example, in an
unofficial strike), strikers may resort to various forms of
social ostracism to punish non-strikers – the device used by
all small communities to enforce conformity on their members. They may 'send to Coventry' a non-striker; that is,
refuse to speak to him, or generally refuse to co-operate
with him and help him out in the many opportunities for
such action that occur among a group of work colleagues.
Behind these sanctions lies the powerful social norm
against 'black-legging' – doing a striker's work – which is
developed within all unionized communities.

Another strategy open to a union is to reduce the employer's power to impose sanctions on strikers. One factor
which heavily determines this is the level of unemployment
in the occupation concerned; the higher the number of
unemployed workers, the easier it is for the employer to
replace strikers. Unions cannot directly affect the level of
unemployment but, for this and many other reasons, unions

have the achievement of full employment as one of the main priorities of their political demands. If there is a low level of unemployment in the relevant trade, it is very difficult for an employer to threaten to dismiss all strikers; even if there is the possibility of replacing an entire workforce, the employer may balk at the disruption involved. In most circumstances he is more likely to try to isolate some workers whom he considers have fomented the strike and discipline them alone. Unions respond to this by threatening further strikes if there is any such victimization; an agreement on 'no victimization' may be one of the union's conditions for a settlement to end a strike. Alternatively (or in addition), unions may seek legal safeguards to prevent the dismissal of union activists. British unions did not demand such protection until the early 1970s, when some provision for the protection from dismissal of workers on grounds of involvement in union work was included in the 1974 Trade Union and Labour Relations Act. Whether this could protect someone dismissed for organizing unofficial strikes is doubtful, because an employer could claim that the worker was unreasonably disrupting his business. The only really effective defence for a union activist threatened with dismissal is the willingness of his workmates to strike for him; there are many examples of this happening, but there are also many examples of workers deciding either that the man was a 'trouble-maker' whom they would sooner be without, or that it is not worth their while losing pay during a strike over one man. For an activist who is dismissed the outlook can be very bleak, whatever the level of unemployment in his occupation. Employers maintain 'blacklists' of such workers, and they exchange such lists with one another and often with the police. Such a worker is therefore highly unlikely to secure alternative employment, unless he is willing to move to another part of the country or completely to change his occupation. Such practices are widespread among employers and are a highly effective sanction, though they receive far less publicity than the equivalent union sanction of refusal to allow a person who either will not join or has been expelled from a union to secure a job.

A further device which is used by workers, both to ensure strength of support among the existing workforce and to prevent the hiring of replacements for strikers, is the picket – the posting of men at the factory gates to limit the chances that other workers will enter in order to go to work. The history of picketing has been a controversial one; obviously the most effective means which pickets can use to achieve their aim is physically to prevent non-strikers from entering the plant. However, this immediately involves a potential clash with ordinary criminal laws preventing violence and threats of violence against persons. Such was often the case in nineteenth- and early twentieth-century disputes. For a long time in the post-war period the number of cases of picketing which involved active police intervention became very small, but in the past decade or so this, like so many aspects of industrial conflict, has become more problematic. In 1972 building workers developed what became known as the 'flying picket'; groups of workers who travelled across the country to sites where work was known to be taking place during a strike, and who used fairly violent methods to ensure that it stopped – facing on the way at least equal violence from the men who had been hired by the employers. Later the same year the coal miners used 'mass picketing' to prevent the delivery of coal (or sometimes of oil) to gas works and power stations; vast numbers of miners and sympathizers stood outside the gates of the works in question, physically preventing the passage of delivery lorries through the gates. Mass picketing was also used during the strikes in road haulage and in local government and the health service in winter 1979. An important feature of the road-haulage strike was the use of pickets to prevent the movement of lorries owned by firms not involved in the strike, particularly those in the food industry. The strike concerned rates of pay in the general haulage industry, that is, the employees of firms specializing in the general carriage of goods for contract; not the fleets of lorries owned by manufacturing, wholesaling or retailing firms themselves. But the lorries of the latter group were picketed, in order to increase the general effectiveness of a strike of lorry drivers, with the intention that either these third-party companies would put pressure on the road-haulage firms to settle or, perhaps more important, that the government, against whose incomes policy the strike was taking place, would intervene to help a generous settlement in view of the threat posed to the supply of goods in the country.

For reasons already mentioned, massive or violent picketing is always liable to come up against ordinary criminal law. The legal controls have been made even tighter in the Employment Act 1980, which limits severely the number of persons allowed to take part in a picket on any one factory, and limits the right to picket to places and workers immediately affected by a dispute. These new limitations are highly controversial. On the one hand, the idea that massive numbers should be used to intimidate people who want to work is repugnant to most people's ideas of freedom. On the other hand, if pickets have no ability to threaten and cajole, they are at a considerable disadvantage. Existing law is highly unrealistic; it provides that pickets shall be allowed in a small number, enough to reason with and try to persuade non-strikers to join them. This implies that in some way the choice whether or not to strike is some balanced decision that a worker must be able to reach rationally and without undue pressure. But this omits the fact that if the worker defies the picket and goes to work he gets his wages, while if he joins the strike he forfeits his wages. If those who claim to be worried about intimidation by pickets really were concerned to ensure that each worker were able to make a rational choice about striking, they would also want to provide that strikers should not lose any pay during a strike, or that those workers who work during a strike should not be paid for doing so! This point is another reminder of the in-built advantages of the employer's position in all industrial relations unless exceptional action is taken by unions to combat it.

Particularly controversial are actions taken by groups of workers not involved in a dispute to help those who are. Secondary picketing is an example, so are sympathy strikes or the imposition on other firms of a boycott of supplies to or purchases from the employer in dispute. To the outside observer these often seem like outrageous interference and pressure, and the Employment Acts of 1980 and 1982 have made nearly all such activity illegal. For unions, however, such action is simply an extension of the central rationale for combination itself: borrowed strength. Through combination workers help each other mitigate the disadvantages of their implicit subordination to the employer, and from their point of view there is little reason why the capacity to borrow each other's strength in time of need should be limited to those immediately involved; to argue that it should is rather like arguing that only earthquake victims should be allowed to help other earthquake victims. It may, of course, be argued that the strength of organized labour which secondary action makes possible reduces national economic efficiency; that has to be demonstrated and is a pragmatic case. It still affords little reason for *moral* outrage at such actions.

The success of the mass picketing of the mid-1970s in a few disputes led the more militant sections of the labour movement to take an exaggerated view of its possibilities. This became evident in 1977 during the strike at the Grunwick laboratories in Brent, London, described in chapter 2. The workers and many sympathizers staged a mass picket outside the works for a prolonged period, almost bringing it to a halt. However, they had made their move before the establishment of any traditions of trade unionism at the firm, and they were able to make very little progress with those workers who were not part of the original dispute and who continued working. The mass pickets were effective, but were more than equalled in strength by the large numbers of police deployed to keep

Figure 3.4 Average duration of industrial disputes, 1960–80, United Kingdom

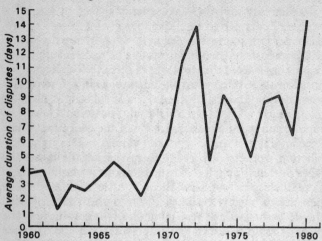

Source: *Department of Employment Gazette*

them back (Rogaly, 1977). In such circumstances it is doubtful if a body of strikers and their sympathizers could ever marshal enough counter-strength if they do not start with the wholehearted support of most of the workers involved.

The tendency for picketing to become more aggressive over the past decade or so in Britain is possibly explicable in terms of the clear trend towards longer disputes, revealed by figure 3.4. The longer a dispute lasts, the more it becomes a real trial of strength, and the more the employer may try to maintain production with a labour force of non-strikers, the more important it is from the strikers' point of view to prevent him from doing that. Further, the increased length of strikes is partly a result of the greater government involvement in industrial relations which has occurred – through incomes policy and through political decisions over the financing of nationalized industries and public services to enable them to meet wage increases. When this is the case, the employer's resistance is stiffened by government policy and is not simply the result of business calculation; this may lead to longer strikes. In such a situation the workers need to put pressure on government as well as on the employer; one means of doing this is to raise a general threat to social order (for which government is responsible) by mounting massive, semi-violent picketing.

Action short of a strike

There are forms of organized disruption available to workers which do not involve the same loss of earnings incurred by a strike (Batstone *et al.*, 1978: 41–4; Clegg, 1979: 258–60). They may merely ban some kinds of work, such as overtime, or they may work more slowly, whether by working 'to rule' or 'without imagination' or some similar device. Such devices are therefore useful to unions in considerably improving the workers' resistance curve, as they become almost impervious to prolongation of the dispute. There are, however, two disadvantages of such action which explain why it is not universally adopted instead of the straight strike. First, not all workers have easy access to such measures, because not all work is sufficiently under the control of the workers – and where it is, pay is likely to be related to workspeed. Similarly, overtime bans involve loss of overtime pay. Second, since the disruption to production is usually less than that of a full strike, the employer's resistance curve is also improved, though perhaps not so much as the workers'. But in some instances these measures short of a strike can be devastating. For example, if a plant's working methods depend on the men on one shift doing overtime in order to make ready for the next shift, an overtime ban by the former may leave the plant in a state where the second shift is unable to start work, with cumulative delays. When the government imposed a three-day week on nearly all British industry in December 1973 it did so because of an overtime ban, not a strike, by the National Union of Mineworkers. It was the three-day week itself which led the union to call a full strike. This was because the reduced energy-demand postponed the point at which the country would be virtually without fuel, strengthening the government's resistance curve (albeit in a self-destructive way).

A similar device which also reduces the cost of a strike is the calling of selective strikes: only some workers within the group involved in the dispute, perhaps those most strategically placed, are called out while the rest continue working. The point here is that the union can keep a small number of strikers on very high strike pay, perhaps helped by special levies on the other workers affected, which it could not afford for the whole membership. Strikes of this kind have been used several times by the teachers' unions, who are perhaps uncertain of their members' willingness to lose pay while on strike. The problems with this approach are that it may impose considerable strain on a minority of workers in key positions, who may be victimized for the part they have played, and it may cause far less disruption than an all-out strike, strengthening the employer's capacity to resist. An example of the former problem occurred in 1971, when the Union of Post-Office Workers launched a lengthy all-out strike which cost the union large sums in strike pay, payments which it was eventually unable to sustain. Many critics of the union said at the time that the union was foolish to try something so expensive as an all-out strike; it should have restricted the strike to a small number of telephone switchboard operators, who could have had a more devastating effect on communications than large numbers of postmen. However, these switchboard workers, the majority of them women, were the least wholehearted supporters of the strike within the workforce, and it was very doubtful indeed whether they would have agreed to be the spearhead of the union's attack.

A variant of the selective strike which is used by unions in Italy and France is a pattern of very short strikes involving different groups of workers, following consecutively on each other (Regalia *et al.*, 1978). This can cause rapid dislocation to a firm's output, even though individual employees are asked to make only a small contribution. Alternatively, the whole plant may be called out, but for a short period of time, say one hour: enough to cause chaos to an integrated production line but not enough to cause material loss of earnings to the workers. The fact that these forms of action predominate in France and Italy is significant: these are countries in which the unions have had low membership levels and inadequate resources to pay strike benefit, and where employers have had reason to doubt the unions' ability to command the loyalty of the workers. These forms of action make a minimal call on workers' sacrifices, while demonstrating considerable organizing ability on the part of the unions.

Strikes in the public service

So far we have assumed that the employer is a profit-maximizing capitalist who loses revenue from orders uncompleted as the duration of a strike proceeds. The situation of a nationalized industry is very similar since it also needs constant revenue from its operations if it is to stay within the financial targets laid down by government. However, many of the public services controlled by national and local government are in a different category in that their income does not derive immediately from the provision of the service. For example, if dustmen go on strike the local authorities do not return to ratepayers the rates they have collected to finance the refuse-collection services; in fact, they *save* money during a strike since they do not pay dustmen's wages while the authorities' incomes are largely unaffected. Does this mean that in many public services the employer's resistance curve is infinite; that is, that the employer is indifferent to a strike by its workers?

The public services almost invariably provide basic needs for which there is a widespread public demand – if they do not meet this criterion they are likely to be abolished as expensive luxuries. There is therefore pressure on the employer to avoid disputes, but it is political rather than economic pressure; if the strike continues there will be public pressure for restoration of the struck service. In several cases, such as dustmen, firemen, hospital service, etc., these pressures can be very severe indeed.

In these cases, then, the workers' strike curve is similar to that of the industrial worker: they have to balance income forgone with the possibility of higher incomes to be gained. The employer's, however, is made up of quite different ingredients: the cost of the concessions needed to end the strike set against the risk of a political crisis. This logic of action may in certain special cases also apply to strikes in private industry; workers who are to be made redundant, or whose plants are to be closed, sometimes strike in opposition to the closure plans, or occupy the factory in a sit-in. There were many cases of this, in Britain and elsewhere, in the early 1970s. Now, on the face of it a strike by workers about to be made redundant is a nonsense; the firm *wants* to dispense with their labour. Such strikes, or sit-ins, are therefore not directed against the employer, but are essentially political acts to try to persuade the government to intervene. As Pizzorno puts it (1978: 279):

A factory decides to close. Although the market power of the workers affected is then by definition nil, since there is no demand for their services, they or their union take an action which obtains some total or partial revision of the management decision. How is this possible? The answer is often in terms of political pressure or political power exercised by the union. Some gain has been obtained in exchange for something 'political'. What kind of exchange is then taking place here? What kind of goods are being traded in this political market? While in the atomistic market more gains were obtained in exchange for more effort, and in the collective bargaining in exchange for continuity of work, in the political market the resource given in exchange may be called consensus or support. An actor (generally the government) which has goods to give is ready to trade them in exchange for social consensus with an actor who can threaten to withdraw that consensus (or, which is more or less the same, to endanger order) unless he receives the goods he needs. In a situation of pure collective bargaining, industrial action means threat to withdraw continuity of work. The exchange becomes political when the threat is withdrawal of the wider social consensus or social order.

On some occasions both a straightforward employer-interest *and* a political interest is at stake. For example, for many years governments have been concerned at the threat to public order and social stability posed by industrial disputes, and the old Ministry of Labour (now called the Department of Employment) always had as one of its tasks mediation between employers and unions in disputes, persuading them to accept compromises. This can be seen as a pressure on employers to make greater concessions than they would willingly have done; pressure imposed by a public authority whose strike resistance curve, based on fears of public order, may have a steeper slope than that of the employers. Alternatively, there have been cases when governments have tried to *stiffen* employers' resistance to pay demands, that is, during periods of incomes policy. In these cases the public authority, which is responsible for overall national economic management, is more prepared to resist pay claims than are individual employers who perhaps feel they can easily pass on the cost of a pay rise in rising prices. Here the government has a less steep resistance curve than the employers and tries, whether through persuasion or legislation, to impose its curve rather than theirs on the settlement with the unions.

Can we say anything systematic about whose curve will be steeper, that of public authorities or that of private employers? As the two examples quoted immediately above suggest, there are occasions when governments have weaker resistances to union demands, and there are occasions when employers have weaker ones. Many employers and their political spokesmen claim that governments are nearly always weaker, since they do not themselves have to bear the costs of concessions to union demands they either make or allow. But that ignores the fact that the political reputations of governments depend very heavily on economic management and on the price level. We could probably specify the kinds of socio-economic conditions in which governments will have stronger or weaker resistance curves, but beyond that it would not be safe to generalize.

The institutionalization of conflict

As asserted at the outset of this chapter, the strike and related forms of action remain the crucial last resort of unions. But most of the time industrial relations proceed without recourse to action of this kind, and agreements are reached between employers and unions in reasonably amicable ways. There is still conflict, but it is regulated and contained and, most important, it does not spill over from the issues immediately at stake to embrace wider political questions. This process of conflict regulation, which is also found in areas of life other than industrial relations, is part of a wider phenomenon which sociologists have called the 'institutionalization of conflict'. For this to take place in industry both employers and unions have to be willing to accept the right of each other to exist; employers have to bargain within certain rules with unions and must give up the struggle to maintain complete mastery of their workforce. Unions have to accept that they will continue indefinitely to extract concessions from employers, rather than seek the complete abolition of the employment relationship as some of them might have done in their early years.

It is useful to see institutionalization as one way of answering the problem posed earlier in the discussion: if employers and unions both confront a weakening of their position during a strike, why do they not foresee from the outset the point at which they might compromise, and thereby avoid the strike? Under institutionalized conflict they try to do so. While these attempts might fail, they will be more likely to succeed if the parties recognize each other, communicate frequently, agree to limit the scope of their conflict to manageable issues, and establish formal mechanisms for the resolution of disputes.

The concept of institutionalization was used heavily during the 1950s by sociologists and others trying to explain the considerable decline in the level and severity of industrial conflict that had occurred since the Second World War. To understand these writers it is important to see the industrial world through the eyes of that period. In the inter-war years virtually every important industrial society had witnessed enormous and frequently violent conflict between capital and labour. In Germany, Austria, Italy and some other countries there had been open warfare, the distinction between strikes, political struggle and civil war becoming indistinguishable, the outcome being totalitarian fascist regimes that destroyed free trade unions. In North America there had been massive and prolonged strikes, with both sides often using firearms and companies employing armed private police forces. By the 1930s the Scandinavian countries were launched on their now characteristic pattern of highly centralized, peaceful industrial relations. But that had been preceded by years of intense conflict in which industrial demands were linked with political struggles for the extension of the suffrage. In Britain, also, there had been major, politicized conflicts, most prominently the country's only General Strike, in 1926.

Against this background the peaceful state of industrial relations in most Western countries during the 1950s and early 1960s clearly called for explanation. Observers noted that in these societies industrial and political conflicts were becoming separated from each other. Management and unions had come to terms with the fact that they would continue to exist together and must therefore develop rules and customs for regulating their disagreements – a lesson which had been learned much earlier in some countries, especially the United Kingdom, but which had not been very evident during the inter-war years. Behind these changes in industrial relations *per se*, observers also saw a change in class relations; the distinctions between manual workers and employers were no longer so stark; many workers were achieving reasonable levels of prosperity and, perhaps more important, security; and on the employers' side, labour relations were increasingly conducted by professional managers who were prepared to deal with unions.[5] In the USA Harbison (1954) described the changes taking place in industrial relations, making use of the concept of institutionalized conflict; Ross and Hartmann (1960) used similar arguments to account for the apparent 'withering away of the strike' which they observed in most countries outside North America; Lester (1958) claimed that as unions 'matured', so they gave up recourse to open conflict and accepted rule-governed relations with management. Kerr and Siegel (1954), discussing differences in the propensity to strike between different industries, invoked the concept of the 'isolated mass'; those workers most likely to strike were those living in isolated and close-knit communities, cut off from detailed contact with the world outside the occupational community – such as coal miners or dock workers. Such workers were therefore outside the scope of institutions for conflict regulation – and were also in sectors likely to decline in advanced industrial society.

The most precise theoretical formulation of the concept of institutionalized conflict was that of the German sociologist Ralf Dahrendorf (1957), who placed industrial conflict in the context of a general theory of the nature of classes and class conflict in advanced industrial society. This presented a picture of industrial society very different from that anticipated by Marx, who saw conflicts becoming increasingly general and bitter, taking the form of clashes between the two great classes of capital and labour. For Dahrendorf, industrial conflicts had become increasingly specific to particular industrial questions, were being regulated and conducted in a civilized manner, and were specific to individual groups of workers and not open to broad class identification.

It is important to note that Dahrendorf is not talking

about the *elimination* of conflict; very much the reverse. He considered that a society which tried to suppress conflict altogether would build up tensions that eventually exploded in massive divisions. In contrast, under institutionalized conflict antagonistic groups had several opportunities to express conflict but, by doing so on a small scale and within a limited context, they were less likely to build up grievances that eventually became large-scale.

Institutionalization can be seen as a matter of degree. At one extreme there are bitter, violent struggles in which a mass of social issues are combined with industrial griev-ances; here there is virtually no institutionalization, ex-cept to the extent that the antagonists hold back from outright civil war. At the other extreme are highly for-malized bargaining arrangements in which employers and unions together regulate employment conditions in a con-text of wide agreement. The wide space between these extremes is filled by a mass of different kinds of relation-ship, exhibiting different levels and types of institutional-ization. For example, a large industry-level strike with mass picketing and the suspension of negotiations because both sides refuse to consider a compromise is clearly less institutionalized than the second extreme; but it is still institutionalized in comparison with the first – a strike which excludes violence is one which accepts considerable self-regulation over means, and if both sides restrict their action to industrial matters, the dispute is contained within the economic arena.

Beyond bargaining: concertation

I have restricted myself to discussing bargaining arrange-ments as examples of institutionalized conflict. But some industrial relations take a different form. Instead of con-fronting each other 'across the table' with demands and threats of sanctions, seeing their interests as in conflict, managers and union representatives may tackle what they see as common problems, with a mutual interest at stake. The belief that such an arrangement can provide either a supplement or an alternative to bargaining has often led various social actors to establish joint committees, works councils and other devices for consultation and worker participation which will embody the idea. After the First World War a committee of the House of Commons chaired by the Speaker, Mr Whitley, proposed the establishment of consultative committees on these lines throughout Britain in order to reduce the prevailing intense conflict between employers and workers. The plan collapsed as, during the depression, most employers decided that they need not bother with such devices since high unemployment was doing enough to make their workers forget conflict. However, the idea persisted within the public services, where 'Whitley councils' still exist today, though they have become normal collective-bargaining channels. A similar initiative followed the Second World War; committees for 'joint consultation' were established in many industries, and it was generally agreed that this provided a second limb of British industrial relations, equal in importance to, but quite distinct from collective bargaining (see, for example, Flanders and Clegg, 1954). This gradually faded in importance as shop stewards in an increasing range of firms and industries extended collective bargaining to cover many of the issues supposed to be dealt with by joint consultation, though there has been some evidence of a revival during the current recession, significantly as shop stewards' movements have been weakened (*Department of Employment Gazette*, 1981).

Elaborate consultation schemes involving representatives of management and of employees, usually called works councils, exist in some British firms, most noticeably in ICI Ltd, but in most Western European countries these exist as a legal requirement in all factories over a certain size, and employers are required to consult the workforce within this forum on certain prescribed issues. More ambitious schemes for involving workers' representatives in non-conflictual participation are those involving worker-representation on company boards, such as was proposed for Britain, though without practical effect, in the report of the Bullock Committee (Bullock, 1977). In West Germany such a scheme has existed since the 1950s, being strengthened in 1976: worker-representatives comprise up to 50 per cent of the supervisory boards of all companies over a certain size. In that country and in Austria there are also works councils (*Betriebsräte*) which differ from those found elsewhere in Europe in that they comprise worker-representatives alone, not workers and managers; these councils have some significant powers of veto over aspects of management policy, and rights to consultation and the receipt of information over many others.

In each case these participative or consultative forums, to which I shall refer generally as concertation, exist alongside but separate from normal collective bargaining. While the latter deals with wages and conditions and is assumed to involve conflict, the former tackle various issues of company policy, especially those affecting employment and workers' welfare, and are supposed to be free of conflict.

It is an interesting issue of debate whether concertation constitutes a further step along the road towards even more institutionalization of conflict. In terms of Dahrendorf's theory, I think one has to answer no; rather than institutionalizing conflict, these devices try to *exclude* it, at least from those areas which are seen as ripe for consultation or participation rather than bargaining. Worker-representatives with a works council are not empowered to back their demands by strike threats; German *Betriebsräte* are required by law to co-operate with management and are not permitted to call strikes. In Dahrendorf's study of Germany (1965), which is largely a criticism of that country for its continued fear of conflict, he uses the preference for *Mitbestimmung* (that is, co-determination, the principle embodied in both *Betriebsräte* and worker-membership of supervisory boards) as evidence of devices for conflict avoidance rather than institutionalization.

In terms of motives and intentions these differences are very important; and, indeed, behaviour within a works council will often be very different from that within a bargaining meeting. However, matters are often more complicated. Although bargaining is inherently conflictual, that does not necessarily mean that it is always conducted within an atmosphere of hostility and opposition. Management and unions may, for example, agree on certain facts concerning the state of demand for the products of the industry, and this may influence their assessment of the kind of wage increase that is feasible. The extent to which this can happen will depend upon the level of trust existing between management and unions; can the workers trust the employer's figures? The importance of bluff in negotiations and strikes was noted earlier in this chapter. Fox (1974a) has discussed at length different patterns of high and low trust which may exist in industrial relations, and the different kinds of behaviour with which they are associated. Clearly, the higher the trust level in a particular relationship, the more bargaining will be based on shared understandings and may resemble joint consultation.

At the same time, concertation may be less free from bargaining than at first appears. If, as is often the case, the people who participate in the consultative forum are the same people who carry on the bargaining, behaviour in the one body will be affected by that in the other: a worker-representative who finds he cannot get his views accepted in a 'non-conflictual' consultative meeting may give strong hints that this will lead him to take a much tougher line at the bargaining table. German *Betriebsräte* often use their right to exercise veto powers over a restricted number of issues – for example, overtime working – as a bargaining counter to get concessions on issues where they have far weaker powers or none at all. People's ingenuity at finding ways of making bargains and using whatever resources are at hand to exercise some leverage over matters important to them will usually outwit attempts at officially delimiting some areas as open to bargaining and others as closed to it.

I do not want to press this argument to the point where one claims that there is no difference at all between bargaining and concertation. Certainly at the level of national systems there can be considerable differences between situations where a union movement considers it shares some kind of responsibility for economic outcomes with governments and employers, and those where it considers its role to be to get the best possible deal for its members in conflict with the other actors; this is a question to which we shall return in the final chapter. The main point to note here is that the differences between types of system are nothing like as great as immediately appears.

As an issue of trade-union means of action, the difference between these two models presents itself as a dilemma: will more be achieved by staying within a conflictual mould or by trying to develop shared understandings with the employer? The choice will be heavily constrained by the context in which the unions find themselves. In what Fox (1974a) would call low-trust situations, where management and workers have a history of providing each other with minimal information and misleading each other as far as possible, unions are likely to opt for a conflict model; in high-trust contexts there may be greater willingness to risk concertation. In systems in which concertative devices predominate, these are likely to infect conduct in bargaining forums with their typical modes of action; worker-representatives will come to the bargaining table with a background of the many shared understandings they have reached with management. Where a small concertative committee exists within an impressive structure of bargaining, the bargaining partners are likely to use that committee as an extension of all their bargaining activity.

Union representatives usually believe passionately in one or other of these contrasted models. Virtually all British unionists are deeply wedded to the collective-bargaining approach, and treat attempts at concertation as a betrayal of their members; there was, for example, deep suspicion within the unions at the Bullock proposals for workers' participation in management. German unions, on the other hand, while also strongly committed to bargaining, believe they can achieve many things through extensions to *Mitbestimmung*. What probably happens is that unions learn over time how to exercise their influence within whatever system they are presented with. Apart from reforms which appear to them as obviously strengthening their position, attempts at changing that system to something different and unfamiliar will be treated with hostility, as they fear they will be less able to use its institutions. This may happen almost irrespective of the formal type of system. There is some evidence for this in a study of American plant-bargaining by a German sociologist (Herding, 1974). The American unionists were adamant that bargaining and conflict were the only possible approaches to serving their members' interests, and that works councils of the German kind were a sell-out. But Herding found that the kinds of issues being dealt with by the Americans were very similar to those dealt with by works councils; that despite the appearance of conflict, there was a good deal of mutual exchange of understandings; and that there were some issues where the workers might have been able to achieve more through a council device.

These different forms of action can be seen as a continuum as set out in figure 3.5. At one extreme we find concertative devices of the kind discussed above. The other extreme from this is contestation – constant, open, non-institutionalized conflict, where there are no mutual adjustments between employers and employees, but both sides adopt opposed positions and take action to secure the defeat of the other. We do not see many cases of this

Figure 3.5 Degrees of conflict embodied in forms and strategies of industrial relations

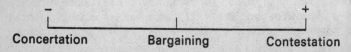

| Concertation | Bargaining | Contestation |

nowadays in Britain, but elsewhere and at other times there have been plenty of examples. Early French trade unions made no attempt to come to the bargaining table with employers; they would call a strike and advertise their demands by parading round the works with banners proclaiming them (Shorter and Tilly, 1974: 35). For their part, employers refused to recognize any representative body among their workers; if they wanted to make concessions to a strike they would merely erect a notice indicating that, say, new rates of pay would now be offered, maintaining the fiction that they had not been forced to have dealings with the union. French industrial relations have still not entirely forsaken this pattern. Many employers take a stand in principle against recognizing unions, and union radicals reject the assumption epitomized in British and North American unionism that what unions do is to bargain. For them bargaining (a word which, incidentally, they usually leave in English to indicate its alien status) is virtually indistinguishable from what I have here called concertation, as it implies accepting the existence of the employer as a continuing partner rather than as a class enemy who should be destroyed as a social category. This can be mere rhetoric but if, as is often the case in France, there are really no institutions within which employers and unions come together in a routine way, then we may talk seriously of a contestative form of industrial relations, implying conflict with very low institutionalization.

If concertation and contestation constitute extremes in the extent to which industrial relations are seen as inherently conflictual, bargaining is located between them; where there is institutionalization, mutual acceptance of each other's permanency, routine exchanges, there is considerable movement away from the contestative extreme. Against the French radicals I would, however, contend that this is also different from the concertative extreme; there are still 'two sides', who exchange concessions and threats within what they see as essentially a 'zero-sum' game, and who treat their interests as being in conflict, albeit of an institutionalized kind within a framework of co-existence.

These have, it should be noted, been described as differences of *form*, of the pattern of institutions, perhaps of their legal stipulation. The same terms can also be used to describe differences of *strategy*, of the different approaches to industrial relations adopted by unions and employers. It is very important *not* to assume that form implies strategy. Social actors often have to accept the particular set of institutions, with their implied logic, which they find already extant within their field of operation; but they may try to pursue a very different kind of strategy within that form, using their skill to subvert it. The case of the German *Betriebsräte* that use the concertative framework of *Mitbestimmung* in order to pursue a bargaining strategy is an excellent case in point. Occasionally one may find also British union representatives who, despite the essentially bargained nature of their system, find they can achieve most progress on a particular issue by seeking a mutually advantageous solution with management, i.e., a concertative approach. (Alternatively, of course, the union official may be inveigled by management into adopting concertation when in fact a bargaining strategy would suit his members better.)

I would argue that there is a general tendency, whatever the formal position, for unions to adopt bargaining strategies, that is, to operate in the heartland of institutionalized conflict, though it must be made clear that 'general tendency' is very different from 'iron law'. Contestation as a union strategy is likely to be an expression of weakness, a response to the refusal of employers to have anything to do with unions; as soon as the employer is willing to make some gesture towards coming to terms with the union, the latter is likely to be interested in the concessions available. The problem with concertation is that, the management being in control of the routine operation of the business, it is only by raising the possibility of withholding co-operation from that routine that a union can exercise some strength; too much acceptance of concertation involves simply accepting management's lead. Trade unions are irredeemable bargainers. However, the force of that tendency may be mitigated, as discussed above, by the historical practices with which the movement is familiar, and also by the opportunities presented at any particular moment; a union bedevilled by low trust in its relations with management, constantly receiving from it misleading information, may welcome some shift to a concertative framework if that means better access to the facts about the company or industry.

Criticisms of institutionalization theory

Most critics would probably accept that the model of institutionalized conflict, as a theory of how social relations might be conducted, was well constructed, and most would probably agree that it provides a reasonable account of what had happened to industrial relations by the 1950s. Criticisms of the theory concentrate on two major points: (i) the assertion by most theorists that institutionalization represents some kind of achievement for all parties concerned, that is, that it is an efficient means for the realization of goals for labour and capital alike; and (ii) the assumption, if such there be, that arrangements of that kind would last indefinitely. On both points the criticisms come primarily from a Marxist perspective.

The first question is an important one for this book: are unions being rational in accepting the domestication of conflict which institutionalization implies, or are they better advised to seek more aggressive and frequent strikes? For Marxists, since capital and labour are seen as irreconcilably opposed interests, labour is not realizing its best interests if it accepts institutional arrangements, since these help stabilize the existing system of work relations and provide no chance for a revolutionary challenge to the very existence of the employer. Certainly, if the rational goal for labour is transcendence of the capitalist mode of production by militant action, then working within the negotiating system of institutionalized conflict does not represent a rational means. But what *is* a rational goal for labour? This is the question we shall address in the next chapter.

Temporarily accepting the Marxist position on this, we see that institutionalization constitutes a betrayal of the workers' best interests. In Hyman's (1972) account the establishment of formal means of conflict regulation usually depends on the detachment of a union leadership from its task of representing the members and its co-optation by a ruling elite. This raises the whole issue of relations between unions and their members, which is the subject of chapter 5.

But, turning to the second aspect of Marxist criticism of institutionalization theory, class antagonism is so fundamental to capitalist society that, they argue, it cannot be indefinitely diverted by such devices. In any case, the contradictions at the heart of capitalism, such as the falling rate of profit, must irretrievably worsen as time passes. As Hyman (1972: 84, 85) says, institutionalization often fails, and the years since the late 1960s have been a major example of such a failure:

> If industrial conflict has shown such resistance to permanent domestication, the presumption must be that there exist powerful underlying causes. To diagnose these causes necessitates an interpretation of the basic structural realities of our society. Such an analysis is inevitably controversial; but it is essential if any explanation is to be given of the continuing prevalence of the strike and related activities in modern society.
>
> Unquestionably the most important point to be emphasized is that class divisions are fundamental to our social structure. . . .

He goes on to delineate the ways in which these class divisions affect industrial relations, through stark inequalities of wealth and income distribution, through conflicts over the control of human labour, through the alienation of workers forced to accept dehumanizing work. So long as these conditions exist, there will always be scope for real, open conflict between workers and those who exploit them. Workers' leaders may be tempted into cosy, rule-governed relationships; workers themselves may be deflected from pursuit of their true interests by skilful ideology; but the divisions are too fundamental to be concealed indefinitely.

The argument that the employment relationship can never be drained of conflict is a powerful one, and one that such a theorist as Dahrendorf would wholeheartedly accept. Where he and the Marxists differ is over the likelihood of that conflict being confined to specific employment griev-ances. Here a crucial part of the institutionalization thesis was that industry, or occupational life, is no longer central to people's lives (Dahrendorf, 1957: 267–72), and, in par-ticular, that it can be divorced from political conflict (*ibid*: 275, 276). The Marxists have the better of the argument here. In all present societies, and for as far into the future as we can see, most human beings will be dependent on their own or someone else's occupational role for their standard of living;[6] and relationships at work will be central issues in people's lives. The claim that industrial conflict can be insulated from politics also seems poorly conceived, though not necessarily on the grounds given in the Marxist accounts; this will be the subject of our final chapter. However, whether these conflicts must ultimately take the form of a clear-cut class conflict is another matter; on this question, and on that of whether, as mentioned above, it is in labour's interests to accept or reject institutionalization, the Marxist arguments carry less strength. It is to that issue that we now turn.

4 Union Goals

That workers should organize collectively can be readily explained in terms of their vulnerability as individuals. But what are likely to be the goals of their organizations once they have formed them? One major question raised here is the possibility that the organization as such will develop goals different from those of the individual members themselves; that is the subject of the next chapter. In order to avoid excessive complication, we shall temporarily set these questions aside and assume that there are no major differences between the goals of workers and of unions.

The first possibility which has to be considered is that goals will not develop much further than the initial one implied by the simple act of combination: protection against the vulnerability of the individual employment relationship; that is, a purely defensive posture against the possible actions of the employer, with little attempt at *initiating* anything at all. Defensiveness may seem an odd strategy; it means accepting the conditions found on entering employment, but preventing any worsening of them. Such a goal is entirely relative. For example, if a group of craft workers have been used to controlling their working methods and workspeeds, the theory of defensiveness predicts that they will resist any attempt by the employer slightly to reduce their span of control; while it also predicts that a group of workers who have never enjoyed such controls will never try to secure any. How realistic is such an assumption of defensive relativism? Should we not rather assume that all workers are all the time trying to maximize their job control?

Defensive goals

Relativism may well prevail, and be rational, to the extent that the knowledge available to the workers tells them (correctly or incorrectly) that their bargaining position is weak. They fear that action to improve their position will lose them their jobs, whether as a result of disciplinary action by their employer or as the economic consequences of raising the price of their labour. They have adjusted their standard of living and expectations of improvements in it to the prevailing level. The expected costs of any action to improve the situation seem far higher than any likely gain. In such a context, aggressive, maximizing behaviour should not be expected. But that does not mean that such workers will never try to use their collective strength. The very depth of their adaptation to an existing standard of living may lead them to be fiercely resistant of any attempts to reduce it, say during a recession. Such action may appear from the outside quite irrational: if the workers accepted that there was little point in trying to improve their standard of living during normal trading conditions, why can they not see that it is equally irrational to protect their former standard during deteriorating conditions? However, workers do not necessarily know at what level their income has to rest as the economy deteriorates; indeed, it is unlikely that anybody knows. On the other hand, they do know what they are defending: a whole way of life and accustomed standards of consumption are being threatened; and a way of life already achieved and become habitual will be fought for much more fiercely than the prospect of new gains which have not yet been tasted, let alone become familiar.

This limited kind of union goal has been very important in the history of trade unionism, particularly that of the less skilled, and lies behind the record of the often desperate struggles which predominated in the early twentieth century. The element of desperation can be readily understood when it is realized that the goal of action is not an opportunistic taking advantage of chances, but the very reverse: the defence of an existing standard from attack. For example, the important dispute in the British coal mines in 1921 which lasted from the end of March to the end of June was a lock-out in which the miners were trying to resist a heavy cut in their wages (Pelling, 1976: 165–6). In 1925 the miners were again expected to take a cut in their wages *and* an increase in working hours, and it was this that led to the General Strike of 1926; the miners fought that strike with the defensive slogan, 'Not a penny off the pay, not a second on the day' (*ibid*: 173 ff). Once we understand the meaning for workers' lives of these kinds of struggles, we can readily appreciate the paradox whereby it is the most conservative of goals which evoke the most militant and determined action.

While much trade unionism goes far beyond this pure defensiveness, it remains a crucial *part* of much action, mixing with and sometimes inhibiting, sometimes leading on to, other goals. A very important example can be taken from the shop-floor movement which developed in the munitions and ship-building industries on Clydeside during the First World War. This seemed likely at one stage to develop into the nearest thing to a revolutionary labour movement which this country has known. The workers engaged in a high level of militancy during a world war for which they were producing vital military material; this challenge brought a repressive response from the government, with many activists being imprisoned or deported from the Clydeside area. It was a struggle between, on the one side, a militarized state co-operating closely with private capital and, on the other, a militant shop-floor movement. The shop-floor level of organization had become important because the official union leadership was co-operating in the war effort. And yet, despite these explosive ingredients, the major dispute in which this movement became involved was defensive to the point of conservatism: a protest over the dilution of craft skills by the introduction of unskilled workers, most of whom were women. Because of the manpower shortages of the war, employers and government wanted to increase the number of workers in defence production beyond the level that was possible through the engagement of properly trained craftsmen alone. This threatened the superior labour-market position of the craftsmen and also threatened union control of labour supply.

The radicals who led the movement had been unable to mobilize the workers on a general platform of opposition to the war, while proposals for nationalization of the industry with worker-participation attracted only limited support because they left unresolved the issue of dilution (Hinton, 1973: ch. 4). Ideas for transcending skill barriers between workers by union amalgamations also fell by the wayside because they evaded the crucial question, though they later returned to prominence, not as a grand design for a union of the whole working class, but as a limited scheme for some administratively sensible union mergers (Pribicević, 1959). As Hinton (1973: 161) comments in the course of his detailed study, written albeit from a revolutionary socialist perspective:

... militancy could not easily be developed beyond the protective reflex of a threatened labour aristocracy, and this difficulty was intensified by the lack of organization among the less skilled workers whose co-operation was essential if dilution was to be positively controlled, not merely resisted. ... The Clyde Workers' Committee failed to transcend the objective limitations of its original base, to become an effective vanguard for the local working class as a whole. Even the revolutionaries could not escape the entanglement in the protective reflexes of the craftsmen, and it was a narrow and self-isolating path that they cut through the turmoil on the Clyde.

Appreciation of the importance of defensiveness among

people accustomed to being in positions of weakness and insecurity (the condition of nearly all working people) is also important for an explanation of frequently observed forms of behaviour among organized workers which often seem puzzling and irrational to more comfortably situated observers. For example, in many industries in Britain workers have resisted, with extraordinary success, reductions in manning levels and changes in working practices that might have been expected to accompany the introduction of modern machinery and techniques. But they have done so within industries and factories in which they continue to work with danger, noise and dirt with relatively little protest. At one level it is possible to interpret this as an expression of preference: workers do not care about noise, dirt and danger, but they do care about manning levels and work practices. It is possible that this is true, but we should not regard evidence of practice as necessarily evidence of preference; we must first take into account the greater priority of the goal of maintaining existing gains over that of pursuing new ones.

Even wage claims which are for real increases rather than for the protection of existing living standards may incorporate defensive components of this kind. A major example was the mining dispute of 1973–4, which is generally regarded as having been an example of extreme militancy and ambition, in that it resulted in a very large wage increase as well as the fall of a government (Crouch, 1979: 86–8). However, it is notable that throughout the dispute the argument of miners' leaders concentrated on the way in which miners' pay had slipped down the 'league table' of average *manual* earnings; and their demand was primarily for a restoration of the position they had reached before the decline in their position had set in. The miners did not use the power they wielded to achieve, for example, changes in the subordination of miners to colliery managements or an advance in miners' earnings to bring them closer to the incomes of company directors.

This predominance of defensiveness, conservatism and

relative lack of ambition, not only in trade-union activity but generally in working-class behaviour, has been the subject of much sociological discussion. The most important contribution to its study is W. G. Runciman's *Relative Deprivation and Social Justice* (1966). Its thesis is that it is not the extent of hardship itself which invokes militancy but disappointed expectations of improvement (or of the maintenance of a threatened standard). For example, he points out that during all the sufferings of the inter-war years, the one event that really provoked 'vehement, widespread and successful' discontent (p. 65) was the Unemployment Act 1934, which *reduced* unemployment benefit. Similarly, he comments (*ibid*: 69):

Manual workers certainly felt that they had a claim on the state. But their demand was not 'soak the rich' so much as 'work or maintenance'. It was in terms of working-class comparisons that their deprivations were felt.

The concept of relative deprivation is primarily socialpsychological; it is concerned with the criteria by which people judge their perceptions. But this is not the kind of psychological explanation which needs to imply pathological distortions in perception in order to explain behaviour. We may go further than this and identify other aspects of rational calculation which will lead to a predominant defensiveness in goal-seeking among social actors whose position is characterized by subordination and weakness within the social structure, and by problems of deficient available information.

First is the frequent reference in workers' pay claims to comparisons with the wages of similar groups of workers, rather than the incomes of the very wealthy. Runciman has considerable evidence of this process. The paradoxical result is that, say, a machine-tool operator is likely to become far angrier if he learns that machine-tool operators in a neighbouring factory have received a special overtime bonus than if he learns that the chairman of the company has been given a helicopter for his private use at the expense of the firm. The theory of ideology would explain this in terms of legitimacy; members of society are taught by the ruling values that superior living standards for leading members of the society are just and right. There may be some truth in this, though recent work has thrown doubt on the extent to which one can identify a 'ruling ideology' in modern Britain (Abercrombie, Hill and Turner, 1980). It is unlikely that ideology provides the full explanation, since it leaves out of account the problems of comparisons involved when people try to work out what inequalities are fair, once one assumes that their measuring rod is not going to be arithmetic equality regardless of differences of circumstance. A mass of differences distinguish occupations from one another; how are we to take these into account and quantify them when deciding how our own standard of living should relate to those of others? The only possible starting point is to assume that people in identical circumstances should be on identical incomes. As differences begin to differentiate occupations, so we try to evaluate their possible relevance. Such a process of comparison can continue until the differences become so numerous that we begin to lose our bearings in the task of comparison; we then simply stop and regard the jobs as non-comparable. After all, comparison and contrast can only proceed against a background of similarity. Thus, the machine-tool operator is easily able to deal with the differences that may exist between his position and that of people doing identical work in a neighbouring factory. He may also feel able to judge the occupations of other workers in similar labour markets whose jobs relate to his own. But if he is asked to describe the relationship between his own job and that of, say, a computer programmer, he may find that the points of observable similarity have been so reduced that he has no views at all.

Evidence that people make the most they can of the observable small differences between broadly similar occupations is also available from a recent study of the local labour market for semi- and unskilled workers in Peterborough. The authors found that although the choice of job facing workers in these categories was very small, they responded by making the most of what little was available, magnifying their importance (Blackburn and Mann, 1979: ch. 1).

There is a further reason why we do not need elaborate arguments about ideology to explain the lack of radical ambitions: the demand curve for labour. Employers will be prepared to employ different numbers of workers at different levels of unit labour costs: the higher the wage of each worker, the fewer will be hired. Nearly all union demands involve, at least in the short run, an increase in unit labour costs. In the simplest case, workers will be aware of the existence of some relationship of this kind, but they will not know exactly at what point their demands will trigger labour-shedding. It is therefore rational for them to seek to advance incrementally, pressing small gains and then taking stock of the effect of them on the employer, rather than making massive and radical demands, the result of which they cannot predict. As Perlman (1928: 6) put it, the economic attitudes of manual workers are 'basically determined by a consciousness of scarcity of opportunity'.

In conclusion, an assumption that the most tenacious goal for organized labour will be the defence of existing gains will be a useful starting point for an account of union goals. It leads us to predict stronger struggles in defence of threatened existing gains than in pursuit of new ones. Further, new goals will be adopted in place of old ones only when their relative attractiveness is very high, because unions will set a high price on the risk of novelty.

Revolutionary goals

Defence of existing positions does not exhaust the catalogue of union goals. In due course we shall examine some realistic day-to-day aggressive goals, but first it is useful to set the parameters on likely goals by considering the opposite of the defensiveness which has so far been discussed: organizations of workers as vehicles for revolutionary action.

While this hardly features at all in actual union behaviour, it is occasionally present in labour-movement rhetoric and as a motivation for some union activists; and it is frequently discussed in the sociological literature. This often takes the form of regret for the alleged missed opportunities for revolution in the history of the movement:

> Professions of socialist aims have not been translated into a programme, a strategy and set of tactics, for their implementation. In that sense, it is true, organized labour here has not produced a 'model' for revolution. But of radical opposition to the established order – of dissent from its premises – there is much evidence in the history of British labour.... There were makings of what might have become – and might still become – a revolutionary impulse: grumbling at most times under the surface of accommodation, and erupting at some, though to no effect so far. Working-class resistance here is not as ideologically empty as the thesis of 'bourgeois hegemony' seems to argue. But its ideology of dissent indeed lacks coherent form. [Westergaard and Resler, 1975: 390–1]

The authors are here taking issue with such other Marxists as Perry Anderson (1965), who have argued that it is a peculiarity of the *English* working class that it has been so unrevolutionary. One way of challenging that is to query the achievements of French and Italian labour (the examples most often cited), and to this we shall shortly turn. But some other English Marxists have preferred to point to moments of 'might have been' or 'almost was' in English history:

> ...in 1832 a revolutionary outbreak was averted only at the eleventh hour. There were reasons, but not overwhelming ones, why this was averted. If it had not been, then it is reasonable to suppose that revolution would have precipitated a very rapid process of radicalization.... [Thompson, 1965: 320–1]

It should, however, be pointed out that in the essay from

which that passage comes, Thompson also makes many other points on this general question of the absence of revolutionary attempts by the British working class, including:

... each advance within the framework of capitalism simultaneously involved the working class far more deeply in the *status quo*. As they improved their position by organization, so they became more reluctant to engage in quixotic outbreaks which might jeopardize gains accumulated at such cost. Each assertion of working-class influence within the bourgeois-democratic state machine, simultaneously involved them as partners (even if antagonistic partners) in the running of the machine. [*ibid*: 343–4]

One argument used by Marxists to explain the continuing absence of any significant revolutionary achievement is to blame union *leaders* for frustrating and controlling the rebellious tendencies of their members:

Trade unions may have *originated* as organizations of working people dedicated to militantly representing their interests (which were otherwise ignored), and in some important cases at least, directed ultimately towards transforming capitalist society. Today, however, the unions can be seen to exert constantly a restraining influence upon the workers, and seem to have lost sight of any vision of an alternative socialist society ... unions have now become a component part of that very system of domination – the struggle against which was once the raison d'être of their existence. [Clarke, 1977: 7]

This theme, the betrayal of the labour movement by its leaders, will be taken up in the next chapter, though it should be stressed immediately that Clarke's view of the original role of trade unions differs from that of most historians of the subject, who have stressed the conservative practices of the early craft societies which defended the interests of skilled workers against employers and the unskilled alike (Pelling, 1976). But there is a second argument within Marxism to explain the lack of revolutionary goals among organized workers:

The problem of why the quiescent labour movement has permitted a society to continue unchanged which is based on the ongoing exploitation of workers can only be resolved in terms of the distortion of workers' consciousness by the power which confronts them. The economic and political control of capitalists permits their intellectual and moral control over the rest of society – that is the creation of a dominant ideology, or hegemony. [*ibid*: 15]

The concept of 'false consciousness' is of considerable importance here, since it concerns distortions considered to be taking place in the formulation of workers' goals. The term is often used in common political parlance to refer to someone who has been deluded as to where his best interests lie. This, of course, begs a host of questions as to the identity of one's best interests. But classical Marxism has a more precise formulation than this. At different historical epochs, different social classes have dominated society, subordinating all other classes to their will. During the period between the emergence of a class and its coming into domination, it struggles with other classes, in particular the existing ruling one. The correct strategy for a rising class is therefore to be aware of its own existence as a class and to pursue a course of action which will realize its historical destiny: the collapse of the existing system and the advance of that system of domination represented by the rising class itself. Thus, according to Marx, the rising European bourgeoisie opposed feudal rule and advanced the cause of the market economy and free competition. A class which acts in accordance with the strategy which will realize its eventual domination is showing true consciousness; a rising class which does not realize that it is a class, or which pursues its goals in harmony with, rather than in opposition to, the rules of existing society, is showing false consciousness. It is not so much a question of whether all members of the class personally see things this way; the important point is that they pursue a strategy of action which is consistent with the realization of the eventual domination of their class.

There are great problems in a working class ever doing this. If I am right in having argued that workers' actions will usually be incremental, concerned with short-time advantage within known parameters, it is not surprising that they rarely follow a revolutionary path. This has been a characteristic of trade unionism which has persistently frustrated Marxists, from Marx's own fraught relations with the Victorian English craft societies onwards: indeed, it is the characteristic which Lenin labelled 'economism' or 'trade-union consciousness'. As soon as workers acquire some power, capital makes concessions to them; and given workers' incremental approach, they take the concessions, with the result that their pattern of demands and gains follows the contours of the concessions which capital is able and willing to make – not that of the points which might overthrow capitalism. And given the tendency for unions to resolve their problems of uncertain information about the labour market by clinging to actions familiar to them, they gradually become wedded to that pattern as their own. In this way the labour movements of the advanced capitalist societies have moulded themselves around their various capitals and have reached accommodations with them. Revolutionary strategies are likely to predominate only where capital makes no concessions and presents a front of total resistance – a characteristic unlikely to be displayed by capitalism[1] and more frequently found in autocratic pre-capitalist regimes. The problem then appears of whether labour will be able to launch a confrontation with a powerful social system, with uncertain knowledge of the balance of forces and ignorance as to the outcome. In these circumstances it has usually been desperate workers, with little prospect of gaining marginal reforms and faced with a hopeless present and immediate future, who have been willing to venture revolutionary acts. In terms of a cost-benefit account, desperate workers have little to lose so may be willing to risk much for however vague a hope of ultimate gain. Important examples occurred in Germany in the wake of defeat in the 1914–18 war, when workers tried to improve their own desperate material circumstances and to abolish the authoritarian and militaristic regime which had led them into the war. They supported revolutionary protest movements and established various revolutionary governments. But the prospects for any real material advance were very restricted, and the attempts were all short-lived (Mommsen, 1981).

Marx and Engels's famous call, 'Workers of the world unite! You have nothing to lose but your chains,' was a reasonable statement in terms of rational-choice theory: *if* the only cost to be incurred is *negative* (i.e., the loss of chains), then almost any action must be worthwhile. The problems are, first, that workers in established labour movements have considerably more to lose than chains; and, second, that workers who are truly desperate have so little power that their revolutionary fervour is likely to lead to failure:

Analysis of both the new and the traditional working class has revealed a fatal contradiction within the working-class movement. Those who are most alienated and most desperate are those who are least confident of their ability to change their situation. Those who are most confident in their own powers and clearest in their intentions feel least embattled and disposed towards desperate remedies. We might also add that the most alienated have, objectively, the least to offer society as a whole: in Marx's sense, they are least progressive. Are we to view a revolutionary class as alienated or self-confident? The ambiguity has remained not just in the realm of ideas, but in the material world too. [Mann, 1973: 70]

Runciman (1966: ch. VI) shows how, as unions won some recognition within the system, so their appetite for taking all power within a totally changed society was diminished.

Marxists have responded to the problem of false consciousness in various ways. The most important, as noted in chapter 1, was that of Lenin, who identified the revolutionary party as the group capable of taking strategic action for the long term and therefore that which must be in the vanguard of the workers' movement, if necessary destroying trade-union actions which stood in the way. Others have been more willing to face the problems of the enormous gulf which exists between their expectations and the consciousness actually encountered within the working class, though they usually still take as their *problematique* the explanation of why workers are not revolutionary, as though in the normal run of things one would expect them to be so. Hinton (1973: 335), in the study of Clydeside during and immediately after the First World War, is an example, wrestling as he must with the contradiction between the revolutionary hopes of some of the movement's leaders and the defensive goals of the majority of workers:

> The 'militant craftsman' and the 'revolutionary engineer' certainly describe categorically different states of consciousness; but both states may well have co-existed, and interacted, in the same head ... an interaction was taking place between syndicalist doctrines of workers' control and the non-instrumental aspects of the tradition of craft control. The development of the movement's attitude to workers' control, and of its political consciousness as a whole, can only be understood in the light of this process.

This 'development' is seen as taking the following form:

> The contradiction in the thinking of the movement could survive only because its leaders did not believe themselves to be in a revolutionary situation. Because workers' control was an ultimate goal rather than an immediate demand it was not urgently necessary for the wartime movement to clarify its position. The discussion of transition to socialism thus remained locked in the syndicalist categories that the movement's own practice was helping to undermine. Only after the war was this confusion resolved, when the demand for workers' control was subsumed into the theory of the struggle for soviet power.
> ... The political creativity of this central pillar of the old labour aristocracy flared brilliantly in the final years of its power. Its contribution made possible fundamental innovations in the ideology of the British revolutionary movement. [*ibid*: 336, 337]

The difficulty with this is that it assumes that in the long term a revolutionary consciousness will have emerged from defensive short-term considerations, and in the final sentence the author writes as though a revolutionary movement of substance subsequently developed. But, nearly seventy years after the revolt on the Clyde, we are no nearer the development of such a movement, while the tradition of craft defensiveness lives on, dying only as modern capitalism manages to dispense with workers of this kind. Moving between nostalgia for missed opportunities in the past and hopes for a future development, Marxists remain unwilling to contemplate workers as they actually exist, today.

It may appear that one of the stronger points of Hinton's analysis is his identification of radical impulses alongside and within craft defensiveness. Is this not evidence of a revolutionary consciousness that will eventually emerge? One has to ask here what importance should be placed on the fact that workers may occasionally, and perhaps particularly during moments of conflict, express radical ideas about eventually ridding themselves of control by employers and managers? Workers may also sometimes play with ideas of winning the football pools, owning a sweet and tobacconist's shop or scoring a century for England. We are only entitled to consider these aspirations seriously if they figure consistently in the strategies of action that these people adopt. Given a choice between these and more mundane life-projects, what do they actually *do*? In each generation a small number of persons does try to set up shops, play high-level cricket or work for revolutionary movements,[2] but none of them is sufficiently widespread for us to be able to treat them as generally prevalent. The fact that enough digging around in the recesses of consciousness may bring something of them out of everybody does not need to be taken into account in studies of, respectively, the likely number of attempts to form small businesses, the future supply of professional cricketers or the possibilities of a revolutionary working class. Evidence from banks on the number of serious enquiries for loans to start businesses, from local cricket clubs of trends in the numbers seeking to play for them, and from revolutionary movements of the extent of their active membership will be far better guides. In other words, 'consciousness' deserves to be taken seriously only insofar as it leads to action that commits the actor; or, in the clear if inelegant saying, when people 'put their money where their mouth is'.

One Marxist commentator, in another attempt to grapple with this problem, has written:

> The working class was possessed of a collective consciousness, but it was rooted in the workplace because it was only there that it came up against capitalism as an immediately experienced reality. The social relations of production in particular workplaces generated an 'us' and 'them' consciousness which daily encounters with work discipline and authority served only to reinforce. [Lane, 1974: 268]

But this consciousness, being so heavily rooted in work relations, tended to 'end at the factory gates', leading to no general political mobilization beyond the trade-union context. Indeed, Stewart, Prandy and Blackburn (1980: 147–9) take issue with this interpretation and argue almost the exact reverse:

> The 'them' and 'us', 'rich' and 'poor' oppositions characteristic of the working class are unlikely to relate directly to practical, everyday friction, as Lane suggests, but to a vague general desire for change *which cannot be located in practical action*. There may be occasions, strikes for example, when individual managements can be metaphorically blamed for capitalism, but for the most part the issues of class relations are distinct from the issues of day to day conflict. We are not suggesting that all workers have clear conceptions of the operation of the capitalist system ... but the understandings available for the extension of practical problems are inhibiting and apparently inescapable.
> ... We believe that the workers studied in the research in question accept the facticity of the capitalist system and understand, however vaguely, the external exigencies which

any capitalist undertaking must face. Industrial relations are conducted within that acceptance and involve, for the most part, marginal issues over which the immediate actors are believed to be competent. *The desire for a more just and equitable system does not find resonance in practical possibilities and is relegated to a vague hope of future political change.* [Italics added]

Hinton concludes his book on the Clyde by speaking of the 'ultimate failure of the craft tradition to yield up its revolutionary ore without the clinging dross of exclusiveness' (p. 337). It is a fine metaphor, but one which unfortunately leaves him vulnerable to the charge of seeking 'fool's gold'. What warrants the assumption that the emergence of a revolutionary strategy would have been the 'real thing', the most fruitful and best solution for the workers on the Clyde? How do we know that it would not have led to abject defeat, as it did for the German workers who raised the red flag over the city of Berlin in 1918; or horrifying disillusion, as it did for the revolutionary soviets of Russia after 1917? Only by clinging to the bold assumptions of Marxist theory concerning the necessary development of class forces is it possible to avoid a doubtful answer to that query. It may not just be false consciousness that leads workers to make calculations different from those of that theory when making real decisions in a real society:

... the persistence of working-class loyalty [to social democratic parties] suggests that the alternatives on offer are felt to have even fewer attractions, the revolutionary Marxist alternatives included. It might well be that western workers would find much to agree with in the Marxist critique of social democracy; but with the passage of more than half a century since the first of several experiments in proletarian dictatorship these same workers are now well placed to weigh up the evergreen Marxist claim to be able to offer something in advance of mere social democracy 'next time'. [Parkin, 1979: 202–3]

The British working class has dug itself into a dense network of defensive positions. And if it has refused to move out of them and take up an offensive posture over so many decades, this is not just because of some 'corporate' conservatism but also because of an active rejection of what appeared as the only alternative ideal and strategy – Communism. [Thompson, 1965: 347]

As noted above, some Marxists have tackled the problem by claiming that the absence of revolutionary consciousness is a peculiarity of the English working class, resulting from the fact that it developed before Karl Marx had written his books and was therefore not influenced by his theories in its formative period (Anderson, 1965). This implies an extraordinary degree of intellectualism in the determination of working-class action. It also raises the question of which working-class movements did grow up under the wing of Marxism. The most obvious historical case was Germany, but the distortions of the Nazi period and subsequent division of the country have disturbed the pattern. The most favoured example now is France, and possibly Italy. The revolutionary rhetoric of the French labour movement has been highly attractive to British sociologists:

... the universal axioms of the French revolution were turned by the working class in France against the bourgeoisie which first proclaimed them; they founded a revolutionary ideology directed against the initiators of the revolution. In England, a supine bourgeoisie produced a subordinate proletariat. It handed on no impulse of liberation, no revolutionary values, no universal language. [Anderson, 1965: 36. See also Mann, 1973: ch. 4, though he is more keenly aware of the limitations of focusing on rhetoric and language.]

What such an approach ignores is the remarkable extent to which action fails to match rhetoric in southern European labour movements. In terms of sheer numbers of workers organized, capacity to force concessions from employers, ability to support political parties which gain office, the French and Italian Marxist union movements have the poorest records in advanced industrial Europe. Some observers, noting this, have offered an explanation: the very exclusion of these movements from national participation has prevented them from developing a pattern of behaviour and accompanying ideology of compromise, leaving them better able to develop as revolutionary movements. There is some truth in this. But to make the case involves the implicit recognition that the development of a revolutionary ideology was in the first place a product of labour-movement *weakness*; and this must raise questions about the course which developments would take were these movements to grow stronger. It is notable that as the Italian movement grew in strength after the late 1960s it began to develop a collective-bargaining strategy, union leaders became involved in talks on national economic policy, and the Italian Communist Party came somewhat to resemble a European socialist or social democratic party (Sani, 1979).

The goals of everyday trade unionism

Now that we have examined the possibilities of the outer limits of trade-union action, we shall move on to consider the range of intermediate goals which are more assertive than mere defensiveness but which remain within the parameters of existing social arrangements and which form the stuff of most day-to-day union behaviour. These can be seen as advances out from defensiveness, for this is what union goal-seeking is typically like: cautious, unadventurous, occasionally taking an aggressive plunge forward where it seems that something can safely be achieved. And it is an approach which suits the logic of workers' situation: many of the factors determining their environment are unknown to them; much has to be taken on trust; their position is, always, one of subordination to capital and fear of bumping against a rigorous demand curve for labour.

Even within this contained framework it is possible to see a bewildering variety of union goals: higher wages, reduced working hours, improvements in many different aspects of working conditions, reductions in the degree of supervision, a share in managerial control, increases in manning levels, improvements in work rules. The differences among these can be important to union strategy, and often a conscious choice has to be made among them. For example, should a union try to increase its members' scope for doing overtime work at premium rates, or should it press for the same work to be done through the employment of a larger number of workers? Should a union accept increases in managerial control and a reduction in manning levels in exchange for higher rates of pay – a dilemma faced very directly in what is known as 'productivity bargaining'? Even more frequently, an *implicit* choice has to be made: an increase in wages may be pursued even though it will lead to unemployment for some of the workers concerned; or an improvement in working conditions may mean that less is available for higher wages.

These implicit choices may be unconscious and beyond workers' control. It must be borne in mind that unions have unequal *access* to different goals. A choice of strategy is not just a choice between goals, but a choice between goals *set in the context of the means needed to secure them*. It may often happen that a union pursues a less desired goal because the means available to secure it are less hazardous than those needed for a more desired goal. The result is often peculiar: unions and workers are seen to pursue a strategy which no one really wants. But the alternative may well have been securing no goal at all.

We can show this formally. Figure 4.1 depicts, in line AB, the early part of the workers' resistance curve during conflict discussed in the preceding chapter; that is, the part of the curve during which the workers have some control of the situation and anticipate a certain strike-duration. Their *willingness* to strike will depend on the size of the anticipated gain. If the curve accurately reflects their preference on this, the workers will be indifferent between any combination of strike-length and prospective gain found along the curve. Situations to the left of and above the curve constitute better outcomes for the workers than those on

Figure 4.1 Workers' and employer's strike-preparedness: employer less willing to concede control demands than wage demands

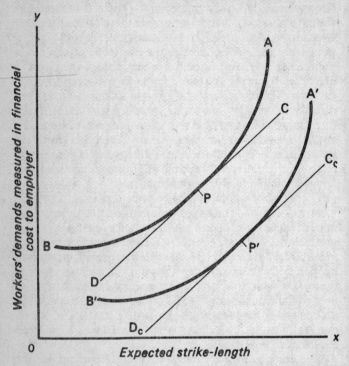

the curve, as they provide a larger gain for a given length of strike. Situations to the right of and below the curve are worse, as they provide a smaller gain for a given length of strike than any point along it. The line CD constitutes the employer's resistance curve for the relevant strike-lengths; agreement between the workers and the employer will be possible at point P.

Now, the y-axis has been described here in terms of the increased cost to the employer of a union demand. In the simplest case this can refer to a straight demand for a pay increase, but it may also be used to describe the cost of other types of demand. Let us assume that the workers want, not increased pay, but various job controls – over the design of work, manning levels and the speed of machines in their shop. Some of these changes have a clearly ascertainable financial cost, while others are more difficult to quantify; but let us assume that the overall cost can be established and that the workers value these changes equally to their cost, that is, that their desire for these changes is equal to their desire for wage improvements of equal cost to their employer. In that case, curve AB will represent the workers' curve irrespective of whether we are talking about wage increases or job controls. However, now let us assume that the employer is very opposed to any concessions on job controls; he may believe that acquiescence here threatens his long-term ability to keep control of his business. Demands for these changes therefore 'cost' him considerably more than the financial cost, and he is willing to concede less in immediate financial terms to reduce conflict over job control than over a straight pay rise. If CD represents his resistance curve where a pay demand is concerned, C_cD_c (parallel to CD but to the right and below) will represent his resistance curve if it is a demand for job control. For such a demand the workers can achieve nothing on AB, but must fall back to A'B', agreement being reached at P'. This gives them less in financial terms for a longer strike if they insist on seeking job control rather than a wage demand, though we have assumed they value them equally. In such a case it will always be rational for the workers to make a pay demand, and they will never get round to seeking job control.

However, over time diminishing returns may set in; repeatedly receiving pay rises but never achieving job-control improvements, the workers may eventually come to regard a given unit of control as more valuable than its equivalent in terms of pay increases. In that case they may decide to seek such demands, even though the employer is willing to concede less in terms of cost-equivalents than for wage demands. However, for this to happen the workers must be more determined to seek job control than the employer is reluctant to concede it – determination and reluctance being measured in terms of willingness to endure a strike for a given unit of cost increase. Two possible situations are presented in figures 4.2 and 4.3. In 4.2 curve A_cB_c represents the workers' resistance curve for job-control demands, AB representing their curve for wage demands, in a situation where they value a given unit of job control higher than a wage demand of equal value in cost

Figure 4.2 Workers' and employer's strike-preparedness: workers prefer job control more than employer is reluctant to concede it

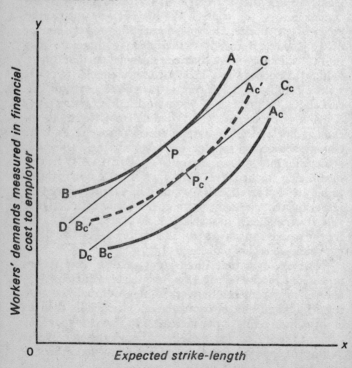

terms; the space between the curves therefore represents the non-pecuniary value of any given control demand across a range of strike-lengths needed to achieve it. CD and C_cD_c represent, as in 4.1, the employer's position where he is, again, more reluctant to concede job control; the space between the lines again shows the non-pecuniary value he places on job control. In 4.2 the gap between the workers' curves is greater than that between the employer's curves, signifying that achieving the job-

Figure 4.3 Workers' and employer's strike-preparedness: workers prefer job control to a wage rise, but by a smaller margin than the employer's reluctance to concede it

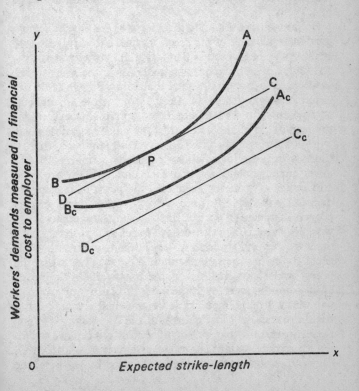

control demand is more important to them than resisting it is to the employer. A deal is available to the workers on a more favourable curve than AB ($A_c'B_c'$), at point P_c'. The gain is worth less in financial terms than the wage rise possible at P, but they take it because of their preference for job-control gains.

Figure 4.3 shows a similar situation, except that the workers' preference for job-control demands is not as strong as the employer's reluctance to concede them, shown by the fact that the gap between the employer's curves is greater than that between theirs. In this situation the workers will go for the wage deal at P, even though they value a given unit of job control higher than a unit of wage rise.

So far we have assumed that the workers are choosing a particular balance of strike effort and substantive goals; strikes have been used as a familiar and suitably quantifiable index of conflict, or more generally of the *effort* which workers have to exert to secure their aims. But we could use several other indicators of effort. For example, for a group of workers who are well organized on a plant basis under the leadership of shop stewards, the most accessible goals will be those which can be achieved at plant level, that is, those within the jurisdiction of foremen, supervisors and lower management. Beyond a certain level in the kind and extent of workers' demands, the point of managerial decision will move to head office, or perhaps to an employers' association outside the company altogether. If the workers want to tackle these levels they will probably have to move beyond their shop-level organization and work through regional or national union officers. The further the point of decision-making on the managerial side moves away from the local level, the more difficulty our group of workers will experience in achieving their demands, and the more they will lose control of the campaign. We may therefore assume that *level of negotiation* can replace strike-length on the *x*-axis of our model as a measure of difficulty. Given that the bigger the demand raised by workers, the higher the level of managerial decision-making is likely to be, the workers' and employer's curves will have a shape similar to those in figures 4.1–4.3. Similarly, it is likely that certain *types* as well as levels of demands will be negotiated at different levels of management. For example, local supervisors may have the power to grant bonuses and minor earnings improvements but not to negotiate changes in working practice (or, perhaps, *vice versa*). In that case, the entire argument around figures 4.1–4.3 can be repeated in terms of negotiation levels rather than strike-lengths, demonstrating that the goals which workers and unions pursue may be determined, not so much by their felt preferences, as by the pattern of opportunities presented to them; workers will secure those goals which are within the easiest reach of negotiation.

Levels of negotiation differ from strike-lengths in one important respect; while strikes may be of a wide range of durations, the pressure on the employer increasing with each day, the number of negotiation levels within an industry will be small, with abrupt changes of negotiable issue at successive levels. Thus it may be that, say, controls over working methods are not negotiable at all except at the highest levels. Sometimes the level of decision-making on an issue may be entirely beyond the reach of any level of union organization, as is the case with several multi-national corporations. In such instances there is just nothing that workers can do to realize the goal in question, however much they want it.

The foregoing analysis has been abstract; no one really makes calculations as fine as those depicted in the figures. Nevertheless, something of this kind goes on every day in industrial relations, every time that a group of workers or a union official decides whether it is worthwhile pursuing a particular issue. In time, people learn that some demands can be successful while others never are; they then stop wasting time making the decision about which goals to pursue and simply take for granted a certain structure of opportunities, unless and until some decisive change in the situation makes it necessary to think again. In this way the particular pattern of trade-union successes and failures in negotiation becomes established. It is just not possible to conclude from that pattern that these were the demands that unions preferred or chose in the sense of being the things they 'really wanted'. Rather, they constitute the results of the clash between what they wanted and what they were able to get, given the preferences of employers and the available structure of negotiation.

It is sometimes argued that British workers have 'chosen' to have a fairly easy workpace in exchange for long working hours and low wages, in contrast with workers in several European countries who seem to have made the opposite 'choice'. But this oversimplifies; no one ever made that choice. What has happened is that workers in several British industries have had the chance to win relatively easy working conditions (workspeeds, manning levels, etc.), offered by the available pattern of negotiation. As a result, less has been available for wage increases. British unions and workers have never been in a position to make a strategic decision to pursue that particular path; no more than were German workers ever in a position freely to *choose* high wages for an intensive workrate.

An analysis of this kind is also useful in comparing the kinds of goal likely to be pursued by workers and unions in different industrial-relations systems. In the above account it has been assumed that the starting point for organization was a group of workers at plant level, and that matters became more difficult for them to negotiate at successively higher levels. This has been the case in, say, the British engineering industry, but in some other sectors, for example, local government, shop-floor organization has until very recently been poorly developed and bargaining has been concentrated on the national level. In such a case those goals which are most attainable are those negotiated between the national union and the employers' association, and issues become less accessible to the workers' side at successively *lower* levels. Particularly striking here are contrasts between the predominant patterns in different countries. The British pattern of some bargaining at plant level and some at industry level is not typical of much of Europe. Historically, it has been more common for employers to succeed in avoiding negotiation with unions except through associations, while at the level of national politics governments were willing to come to terms with unions – either, as in the case of Scandinavia, because parties linked to unions soon became enduring parties of government; or, as in France, because governments feared the threat to social order posed by militant organized labour and wanted to compromise (Shorter and Tilly, 1974).

These differences have led to considerable variations in the achievements typical of different union movements. The unions of Scandinavia and continental Europe have spent considerable energy on establishing a set of legal guarantees for union rights, and have sometimes been willing to accept limitations on their strike freedom in exchange; while British unions have been more concerned to protect their right to wage unimpeded conflict with employers, at the expense of pursuing legal rights. Over time, union officials and activists become accustomed to the particular pattern familiar to them, and given that novelty always involves a cost in terms of the need to obtain information and establish trust, they prefer it to alternatives and identify with it. It may then appear that a particular system looks the way it does because it is a reflection of the views and values of the people working it. But, before we draw such a conclusion we should examine the structural forces which have, over the years, encouraged the apparent choice of a particular pattern.

Substantive and procedural goals

Analysing goals in terms of the structure of opportunities in this way can help us make considerable progress in explaining the objectives selected at a particular time by particular groups of organized labour. But setting all that aside, what theories can we produce to predict unions' selection of objectives when they do have a more or less genuine choice? There is little we can do to distinguish between the mass of possible substantive goals. However, we may make some progress by reducing them to a small number of abstract categories.

Certain American social psychologists have attempted to develop 'hierarchies' of workers' 'needs', asserting that first workers have to satisfy basic material wants like food and shelter, but that after levels of satiation of these have been reached, they seek non-material goals such as job satisfaction and participation (Herzberg, 1966; 1967; Maslow, 1970). But there may be a different, less psychological, more calculative-rational explanation of workers' participation needs, related to the problem of trust which, as we have noted before, is a problem for workers, not because of any emotional need to feel trust, but because of the difficulty in securing reliable information for use in planning collective action. As Fox (1974a) has so clearly demonstrated, trust is frequently in short supply in the capital-labour relationship. This is because the wage-effort bargain is a purely economic one. If the employer offers a wage higher than the market value to him of the worker's services, he will go out of business; if the worker offers more work than represented by his wage, he is a 'mug', since the employer will simply pocket the value of the extra work. Both sides are therefore constrained to give just enough, and no more, to make continuation of the relationship worthwhile. There is no expectation of any gratuitously generous action; there can therefore be no trust. If the employer stops having the workers supervised, trusting that they will continue working as before, he will find that they simply stop work, or work more slowly. Similarly, if the workers increase their effort, trusting that the employer will retrospectively reward them, they will be disappointed. Every demand for a new concession has to be fought every inch of the way.[3]

One of the themes which Fox is demonstrating is that where pure economic exchange exists, workers must be expected to show extreme suspicion towards management and to insist that everything is brought to the bargaining table. This is important to an understanding of union action. Further, workers and unions must try constantly to force open further issues for joint discussion, whether through bargaining or through participation in decision-making. If an issue is left to management to decide, workers will fear that advantage will be taken of them; but if they get the chance to bargain the issue, or at least to glean accurate information on management's decision, they stand a chance of avoiding being 'mugs'. In these circumstances workers may quite rationally decide to seek, not just intrinsically satisfying goals (such as improved wages and conditions), but also the extrinsic end of *controlling the means of securing their intrinsic goals*. In other words, alongside their substantive goals they may seek a procedural one: the right to control, to co-determine, or to bargain every detail of a work relationship. To illustrate the general point with an example: in addition to seeking such an aim as a pay rise, workers may seek to control the *sources* of possible pay rises, perhaps by insisting that shop stewards and not managers have the right to decide and allocate overtime working. And, as future discussion will show, they may sometimes choose to pursue the latter kind of goal at the partial expense of the former.

The procedural goal may take many forms. For many years the original craft unions protected the right of unilateral control, that is, freedom from all managerial interference in job regulation – a right which they have long since lost but which professions like medicine and the law still guard jealously today. Something approximating craft control has been retained by craft workers, and has eventually been won by many semi-skilled workers in such industries as engineering, where, at least until the current recession, management would not dare change manning levels, work-speeds or job classifications without elaborate negotiations

which usually they would prefer not to risk. In other cases
workers simply insist on very detailed bargaining every
time management wants to make a change. A more formal-
ized sharing in control is found in German industry. There,
works councils consisting entirely of worker-representatives have a legal veto over several areas of plant- and
company-level decision-making (such as overtime working, dismissals, certain working conditions) and a right to
share control with management over other issues (such as
redundancies and future employment policy). Further, in
larger German companies workers have up to one-half
representation on the supervisory board of the company,
with the same rights as other directors to information and
decision-making. On a different model again, it is possible
for workers to own and control firms themselves, without
either a capitalist entrepreneur or the state intervening.
This form of ownership is called producers' co-operatives,
and is found in many different countries, though usually
only as a very small component of the total pattern of
employment (Clayre, 1980).

These different forms of worker-participation in control
differ strongly from each other, and trade unionists debate
fiercely their respective merits. However, for present purposes we can treat them all as examples of workers seeking
a goal concerned with *control over* work rather than with the
returns from work. This is a more fundamental distinction
between goals than that between different substantive
goals, such as the choice between higher pay and longer
holidays.

The definition of some union goals as the search for
rights can be subsumed within the more general category
of control: to demand a right rather than a particular
material gain is to demand predictability, assurance, something on which one can insist and, thereby, impart control.
The importance of unions' search for established rights
rather than for immediate material gain was first noted by
the Webbs (1897); it provided for Flanders (1970: 13–47)
his fundamental emphasis on industrial relations, especi-

ally from unions' point of view, as *rule*-making. These
writers and, even more so, Poole (1981: ch. 8), stress the
superior ethical status of demands for rules and rights over
substantive and instrumental goals. This is accurate in the
sense of the ethical as the search for consistent principles
of conduct, but it is doubtful whether either unions or
employers act ethically in the higher sense of pursuing
rules irrespective of whose material interests they serve. If
they are willing to subordinate themselves to a rule, it is
because they calculate that they stand to gain more from its
existence than from its abolition. As Hyman has pointed
out (1975: 12), few industrial-relations actors pursue regulation for its own sake. I prefer to treat the search for
rights and regulation as an aspect of the search for
control.

Matters become particularly interesting when we consider the need for workers sometimes to choose between a
substantive goal and a procedural one. For example, would
workers prefer to earn £100 a week and surrender all
control over work practices, skill designations and manning levels, or earn £70 a week and retain control over
these dimensions? Employers may often decide, rightly or
wrongly, that worker-controlled work is less efficient than
management-controlled work, and therefore be prepared
to pay more for the latter. Often this choice has had to be
made explicitly and starkly by groups of workers. Reference has been made to the practice of productivity bargaining. In its original meaning this term referred to precisely
such an exchange. As described by the main theorist of the
concept, Alan Flanders, productivity bargaining was a
means of tackling the situation in which managements had
gradually lost control over pay and work systems at the
workplace to strong groups of workers represented by
shop stewards (Flanders, 1964). What some managements
did in those circumstances was to draw up a comprehensive
list of work practices they wanted changed and of controls
over the deployment of labour which they wanted to regain.
They then offered to the men and unions concerned in-

creases in wage rates in exchange for concessions by the workers of the points on the list. Sometimes the improved wage rates looked very generous indeed, because it was worth that much to managers to win back control over the conduct of work.

Workers had to choose in a very clear-cut way between their job controls and increased pay. It was not an easy choice. The job controls had been won through prolonged struggle. If they sacrificed these now, would they find that in the long run the management, enjoying its regained powers, would be able to erode the value of the apparently large wage increases initially being offered? Some writers (such as Cliff, 1966) clearly believed that this was likely. On the other hand, some of the areas in which workers had been able to win control represented strange victories, such as the right to work long hours of overtime. The idea of giving these up in exchange for real wages often proved tempting.

Many workers at present working in the public services are likely to be faced by dilemmas of this kind if the present government goes ahead with its hopes of having much work of this type carried out by private sub-contractors rather than by the employees of the public service itself. Major examples are the cleaning of government offices, where privatization is well advanced, and refuse-collection. When these jobs are done by public employees, authorities have to abide by the public service's rules of accepting union membership among the workers and of pursuing policies of consultation and co-operation with unions over manning arrangements. One of the results – indeed, motives – of pushing this kind of work into private sub-contracting is that it can then be done by non-union labour, or at least by firms which grant the union very limited negotiation rights. Working conditions are then beyond the control of the workers. Initially this very fact makes it possible for the firms to pay higher wages than the previous public-service employment. The problem for the workers is: how long will these higher wages survive the final retreat of union representation and of worker control over the use of labour?

Workers' frequent preference for job controls over higher pay but with managerial control is often depicted as one of the main examples of the obtuseness of British trade unionism. In some senses it is: workers say they want more pay, and are often willing to strike for it; but they are not prepared to surrender the working practices which weaken the efficiency of their production and keep their wages low. Meanwhile, the lack of competitiveness of their products, resulting in part from worker control over work practices, leads to the loss of markets for British goods which must eventually lead to unemployment for the very workers who believe they are struggling hard to maintain employment through high manning levels.

But to view matters this way is to ignore the logic of the workers' position: can they *trust* that the high levels of pay initially offered for the loss of control will be maintained in the future? How do they *know* that changes in their working practices will lead to higher levels of efficiency and productivity in the company as a whole, which will in turn lead to better sales, which will in turn again safeguard employment levels? There is 'many a slip 'twixt cup and lip' in that particular chain. Against all this doubt and mistrust they do know as a fair certainty that if they surrender job control now, they will be subject to far more management interference in the ways they do their jobs, their workloads will get heavier, and some of them will be made redundant as surplus labour. Not surprisingly, workers often demand a very high price for the exchange of job control for higher pay, because the price of the concession has to overcome the high element of risk involved (Crouch, 1980).

We can represent the different combinations of substantive and procedural goals which workers may hold on indifference curves, as shown in figure 4.4. The curves AA', BB', CC' represent the workers' preferred combinations of a substantive (pay) goal and a procedural (control) goal

Figure 4.4 Workers' indifference curves, substantive and procedural goals

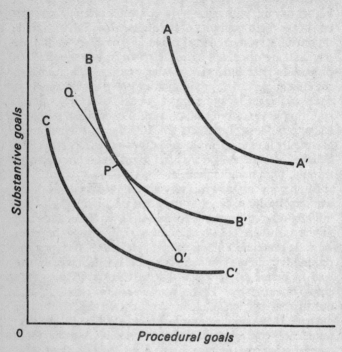

at successively higher levels of bargaining power. The straight line QQ' represents the range of concessions which the employer is willing to make in bargaining. P represents the point at which agreement is likely to be reached on a given combination of substantive and procedural goals at this particular balance of forces.

Now, let us assume that, as a result of certain developments, the workers suddenly have grounds to exercise far less trust than before in their employer. To be sure of straight dealing they now feel they need more control in their own hands. A given unit of control has therefore

Figure 4.5 Workers' indifference curves, indicating a shift in preference towards procedural goals

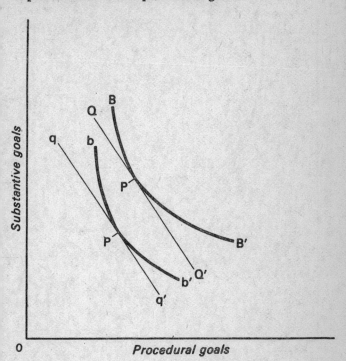

increased in value to them, *and has therefore increased in value relative to a given unit of pay*. This means that they will now be willing to exchange a unit of pay for a *smaller* unit of control than before. Figure 4.5 shows the effect which this shift of preference may have on curve BB', in line bb'. Unless the workers can do something to increase their bargaining strength, moving in the direction of CC' in figure 4.4, the result of this change of preference is to weaken their position. Since they are willing to take smaller amounts of job control in exchange for wage increases, their achievement of substantive goals will be reduced, but

Figure 4.6 Workers' indifference curves, indicating adoption by employer of a productivity bargaining strategy

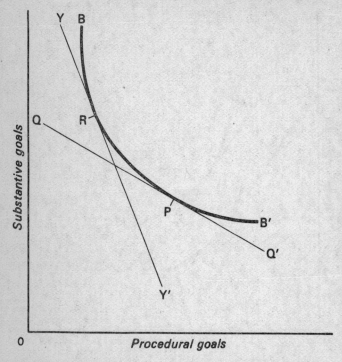

so also will their achievement of the procedural goals they now value so highly. The outcome is therefore a bargain on the less favourable employer curve qq′, at point P.

Alternatively, the particular balance of substantive and procedural goals may change because of a shift in employer strategy. Figure 4.6 shows the effect on bargaining outcomes of an employer adopting a productivity bargaining strategy of the kind outlined by Flanders (1964). QQ′ represents the employer's position before adoption of the strategy. As a result of adopting it he is less willing to concede control demands, and is therefore willing to offer proportionately more pay concessions than procedural concessions in any particular negotiation; his curve moves to something like Y Y'. If the workers' curve continues to take the shape indicated here, a productivity deal will be possible at R.

A paradoxical implication of the above analysis is that weak or non-unionized workers may receive higher wages than unionized ones. This happens in the following way. All workers will from time to time receive pay rises as a result of improvements in productivity,[4] but increases in job controls and similar procedural goals are almost entirely dependent on collective action.[5] The control demand of unorganized workers is therefore very nearly zero. We can turn to any of the employer curves depicted in figures 4.4–4.6 and see that, at very low values for the procedural goal, employers are willing to pay higher wages than at the positions likely to be occupied by organized workers. This very realistic possibility demonstrates the difficulty of trying to estimate the value to workers of union membership by comparing wage rates in unionized and non-unionized firms. Indeed, there are many cases where employers deliberately pay higher rates than those being negotiated by unions in order to dissuade their employees from joining a union. These higher rates may be regarded as the premium the employer pays to prevent encroachments on managerial control.

The conflict between substantive and procedural, or pay and control, goals has been the subject of much discussion in the sociological literature. The latter are usually regarded as more radical, in that they are inherently more political, and because it is thought to be easier for capitalism to make economic concessions than to compromise on the relations of domination and subordination that are so crucial to capitalist economic relations. For example, Giddens has argued (1973: 205):

Struggles over control are 'political' struggles – using this term in a very broad sense – since they necessarily involve attempts on the part of working-class associations to acquire an influence over, or in the most radical context to gain full control over, the 'government' of industry.

It is true, as I have noted above, that the pursuit of control goals implies a degree of organization whereas material gains may be achieved more or less automatically, but this analysis is far less useful than it seems. Both pay and control demands can vary considerably in size. The latter can include small-scale attempts by workers to keep some control over the speed of their machines, as much as dramatic demands for sharing in the control of investment decisions. Minor control demands can be conceded far more easily than ambitious wage demands! Indeed, many British managements seem to have been willing over a number of years to concede fairly extensive workplace controls to the workforce, the latter having enjoyed them at the expense of higher wages. In many respects the argument that control goals are inherently more radical than material goals is a product of the long years of post-war economic growth and prosperity in which the achievement of higher standards of living required far less political struggle than critical observers of capitalist society had envisaged.

Further, in the late 1960s there was considerable interest in an apparent shift from substantive to procedural goals among many workers. The discussion was concentrated on France, where Serge Mallet (1969) had claimed to discern a new concern for control among those whom he called the 'new working class'. By this phrase he denoted those highly qualified employees – technicians, engineers, certain kinds of manager – who wanted to practise their occupational skills as true professionals and resented the authority exercised over them by employers and senior managers who were often ignorant of the science and technology of the work. A related argument was that of Claus Offe (1970), who suggested that with modern industrial processes a change was taking place in the relationship between supervisors and workers. In an earlier period of simpler technology and smaller production units, a worker's supervisor was often himself a man experienced in the worker's own job; at least he knew all about it. Today, however, as techniques have become more specialized, and as special- ized careers in administration have developed, supervisors and managers are often quite ignorant of the work skills of those they supervise (see also Legendre, 1978).

These are serious arguments. Within the areas of tech- nical and expert employment, such as is found in many quasi-professions, they may be very important for indus- trial relations and trade unionism. Workers in these sectors are reaching for some of the autonomy always enjoyed by the old liberal professions, with the difference that their labour-market position is that of salaried employees rather than self-employed fee-earners. As a result, their demand for work autonomy is likely to be channelled through trade unions rather than through professional associations. This demand is certainly political, though there is no reason to assume that capitalist employment relations cannot adjust to absorb it.

However, Mallet and his followers have exaggerated the extent to which these new highly skilled employees can be regarded as some kind of a vanguard for the working class as a whole; if the number of occupations likely to come into this category is limited, then the implications for the overall system will be contained. Indeed, another and currently more fashionable trend in Marxist thought draws attention to a contrary tendency in the development of labour skills, and is just as confident as proponents of the 'new working class' in seeing this as a universal trend. This is the school represented by Henry Braverman's *Labor and Monopoly Capital* (1974), which describes the *de*-skilling of much skilled manual and clerical work in management's drive for greater control (see also Edwards, 1979; and for a more critical view, Hill, 1981). Proponents of the Braverman thesis share with supporters of the Mallet school the view that issues of control constitute the central battleground, but they do not agree on the prognosis of the direction of struggle.

Subsequent research has not supported much of the
Mallet thesis (e.g., Gallie, 1978). Workers often seek control, not because of any determination to seize power over
the system, but simply because for them, *like management*,
control is a means of better guaranteeing their own *material*
goals. If workers can secure control over workspeeds, for
example, they may be able to ensure that the firm nearly
always needs overtime working, which is, of course, paid
at premium rates.

However, the distinction between procedural and substantive remains relevant; as we have seen, workers may
often have to choose between the two. The issue only
becomes unrealistic if we try to link one or other of these
types of goal to a grand design of revolutionary strategy.
Provided we stand within the bounds of realistic trade-
union action, we are unlikely to draw misleadingly
grandiose conclusions or identify doubtful historical
tendencies.

5 The Union as an Organization

So far I have talked of unions as simple collectivities of workers, assuming no problems in a collective's expressing the interests of its members. This assumption is unrealistic and must now be examined. Organizations, whether of workers or of anybody else, are not the simple embodiments of their members' wishes; they are social institutions in their own right, and develop their own internal patterns of power, goal-seeking and conflict. This was a major theme of early twentieth-century sociology. Earlier, nineteenth-century sociology had been preoccupied with the decline of the old religion-bound, rural, aristocratic society and its replacement by individualistic, industrial, bourgeois society; emphasis was placed on the breakdown of traditional ties which had bound men together, leaving them alone and lonely. But as industrialism progressed, as the scale of organizations grew, as the mass of ordinary people began to try to do something about their subordinate predicament within society, so the image of the lonely individual receded. Sociologists took an interest in the phenomenon of large-scale organizations, which were binding men to collectivities again, but in a manner very different from those of traditional society. Here began the sociology of organizations.

A particularly clear if brief formulation of the question is found in Max Weber's (1920: pt. II, ch. IX) distinction between class, status and party. Status referred in the first instance to that automatic correlation between power and acknowledged social rank that characterized aristocracy;

class referred to the inequalities rooted in the possession of material resources, the inequalities distinguishing the isolated individuals of the new bourgeois society; and party was a reference to the phenomenon of organization, whereby the power of a group was dependent on its ability to form combinations which put pressure on the state and other institutions. In Weber's view this was primarily an instrument for those lacking resources of status and class; in other words, the power of party would in the first instance be that of the working class – though there was no reason why privileged groups should not try to strengthen their position further by adding organization to their other advantages.

A central interest of the sociologists concerned the tendency for organizations to develop a life of their own, apart from the membership which created them. Viewed in terms of the Olsonian theory of collective organization, we may see the employment of a specialized staff as one of the ways in which a collective solves the problem of the demands of participation placed on its members. So long as it can extract a membership subscription from them, the organization can employ full-time paid staff to do the work of organizing, discovering information, planning strategy, etc., that would otherwise have to be undertaken by volunteers prey to the dissuasive logic of collective action. The membership thereby solves the problem of its own need to participate, but in so doing may exchange it for another problem. The organization, now seen as consisting of a staff, the 'apparatus', rather than just the members, takes on a life of its own, may become unresponsive to membership demands, and may even come to establish stronger relations and shared interests with the apparatuses of similar organizations of other movements, possibly those of opponents.

Weber had drawn attention to this problem in his study of bureaucracy, and while he was primarily concerned with the way in which, in the modern state, the aristocratic politician was being rendered powerless by the bureaucratic machine created ostensibly to carry out his will, he was also aware of its likely implications for socialist movements. Other writers concentrated more explicitly on organizations of the masses. Mosca (1896) and Pareto (1923) proclaimed the incapacity of the masses to control the organizations created in their name, and developed the idea that, in order to induce participation, leaders would enunciate fraudulent ideologies. Particularly in Pareto's hands, this became also the argument that the masses would be incapable of pursuing, within their organizations, the kind of rationality of means and ends embodied in the capitalist institution of the market; a theme later applied directly to the study of industrial relations by the American social psychologist Elton Mayo (1949). Irrationality appeared again in George Sorel's (1921) volatile doctrine of the confrontation between the mass and the decadent bourgeois society; the masses would be led to organize themselves by their belief in a purifying myth, but this myth had no relation to any rationalistic means-ends scheme – mass collective action was only good for non-rational action.

The Michelsian approach

But most significant for our present purposes was the contribution of Roberto Michels (1915), a pupil of Weber who took up the latter's intimations of the problems which organization and bureaucracy would pose for working-class political parties and trade unions. Focusing his attention on the German Social Democratic Party and its associated trade unions before the First World War, Michels argued that leaders of labour movements would always dominate the membership; whatever the rhetoric of democracy, working-class organizations would be subject to an 'iron law of oligarchy'. This would happen for three main reasons: technical, organizational and psychological. On the first, the leadership, by virtue of its specialized role, would become expert in the technical knowledge needed to conduct the movement's campaigns, and this claim to superior knowledge could be used to refute the arguments of any critics. Second, control over the organizational structure enabled the leaders to ward off challenges to their position from any rivals; the union's press would boost the leader's reputation, and they could use their office to establish patronage for supporters and punish opponents. Finally, and here Michels's argument was far more speculative, the mass membership would identify with their leader and want him to exercise power on their behalf. Not only would leaders in this way distance themselves from membership influence, but would use this distance in order to betray the revolutionary goals of the movement. This was because, as leaders, these men had left the working class and joined the bourgeoisie; they would therefore not pursue policies which would undermine bourgeois status and privilege. Michels was writing as a revolutionary socialist, though later in his life, in the depths of his cynical disillusion, he (like Pareto) became a supporter of Mussolini, whose fascist party unashamedly rejected all pretensions of democracy and proclaimed the domination of the masses by their leaders.

The Germany in which Michels's labour movement existed was not a democracy but an authoritarian regime (*der Obrigkeitstaat*) under which unions led a cat-and-mouse life in their relations with the state while socialist parties had for a time been illegal. It is surprising that a theory about the internal structure of parties and unions forged in that situation should have been enlarged into a *general* theory about labour parties and trade unions, and one which has dominated the literature of labour movements in democracies ever since. There have, nevertheless, been many cases of major trade-union figures who have seemed to fit Michels's mould. Martin (1978: 103), before going on to argue that by the late 1960s matters had begun to change, comments on the usefulness of a Michelsian approach before then:

In the mid-1950s, especially in the United States, it may have been realistic to depict central domination as the norm, with autocrats like Lewis (Mineworkers) and Reuther (UAW) in the United States, Deakin (TGWU) and Williamson (NUGMW) in Britain, and Otto Brenner (IG Metall) in Germany dominating their respective movements.

And so most investigations took Michels as their starting point. For example, a major American study in the 1950s, which has itself become a classic of the literature, argued that the Michelsian hypothesis of an inevitable oligarchy in mass organizations was valid except in the very special and rare case of unions which permitted the formal operation of rival 'parties' within the one union (Lipset *et al.*, 1956).[1] The authors found a remarkable instance of such a phenomenon in the US Typographical Union.

However, as Martin continues:

By the late 1960s the situation had changed. Even in the United States, significant opposition groups had emerged in numerous unions, including the UAW, the Mineworkers, the Steelworkers, the National Maritime Union, the Teamsters, and the Painters; tension between important locals and head office had become apparent, for example in the UAW over the significance of job control issues.... There is even evidence of opposition candidates winning union elections.... Oligarchic domination is even less evident in European unions. Although the turnover in elected union officials has remained small, economic, normative and political changes have reduced the ability of union executives to guarantee compliance. The iron law of oligarchy operated under specific historical conditions which have since disappeared....

This suggests that the search for checks to oligarchy should move away from the stringent demands for formal intra-union party organization established by Lipset *et al.*, but recent American research continues to look primarily at the scope for *electoral* devices. The most sophisticated example, by Edelstein and Warner (1975), attempts to measure the degree of oligarchy in unions by considering the closeness of election results and the frequency of defeats of incumbent or favourite candidates. But the question whether or not a union leader can ride roughshod over the views of his members, or whether groups within the union can act autonomously, are not decided by the fact of competitive elections alone, but by the day-to-day pattern of interdependency between leaders, members and lower-tier officials. An important statement of this case has been made by Hyman (1971), who points to the development, in Britain and elsewhere, of autonomous shop-floor movements with a capacity to wage their own conflicts, and the evidence that union leaders are often obliged to follow and ratify the actions of these groups. Indeed, Hyman points out that leaders may actually *want* to follow their members' wishes! Contrary to Michels's belief in the psychological dependence of members on leader domination, there is considerable evidence, at least in Britain, of members being very reluctant to allow any privileges to union officials. Even in the USA, where there is less stress on democracy and equality in the labour movement, the logic of 'business unionism' still implies that leaders must deliver something to the members to retain their loyalty. Similar arguments are presented by Martin (1968 and 1978) from the point of view of the non-Marxist British sociological tradition; he takes issue with Michels's bald assertion that the leadership always wins conflicts with the rank-and-file, examining the economic, political, organizational and normative variables which in practice produce very different outcomes to these conflicts.

We can express some of these criticisms of the Michelsian approach more formally, by taking advantage of a recent attempt (Child, Loveridge and Warner, 1973) at providing a theory of trade unions as organizations. This distinguishes between two tasks of unions. First, as membership associations they have to represent their members' interests, otherwise there is no reason why anyone should join in the first place. Second, like all organizations, the union will want to carry out its defined tasks effectively, which means it needs an efficient administrative system.

The problem, the authors argue, is that often what they term the two 'rationalities' (of representation and of administration) conflict. We have encountered something of this problem before, in chapter 2, when we discussed the arguments of Offe and Wiesenthal (1980). They maintained that a difficulty facing organizations of labour (as opposed to capital) was that the particular wishes and demands of the mass of individual members were not obvious or unanimous, necessitating procedures for aggregating and deciding on union strategy. Child *et al.* put the point somewhat differently. Administrative rationality

is the design of organization in such a way that specified tasks or outcomes are attained with certainty and economy. These conditions appear in many instances to require a routinization of operations, specialization of functions, directness of communication, and speed in decision-making. [p. 77]

The conflict between this and representative rationality is clear:

Representative rationality emphasizes, in contrast, a flexibility of operations to suit the needs of different membership groups located within different working situations, a duplication of functions in order to build checks and balances into union control, a multiplicity of communications in order to allow the maximum possible interchange and collation of opinion, and a holding back of decision-making until every viewpoint has been expressed. [*ibid*]

But the conflict is not total. The authors suggest that very small unions might combine a highly democratic system with an immediacy of execution while very large unions may not only have difficulties being representative, but may also become clumsy and inefficient. This condition apart, one might assume that unions will, given the constraints on them, try to reach some kind of balance between the two rationalities rather than maximize either of them at the expense of the other: what is the point of a wonderfully representative system if it can never put its democratically assembled views into practice; what is the point of a superbly efficient organization that does not know what it is meant to be using its efficiency for? However, if we follow Michels's account, a different element enters. Administrative rationality is one of the devices that strengthens the leadership, as it helps establish an organizational bureaucracy which the leader uses to buttress his own position. The motive for constructing administrative rationality becomes, in this account, not the better conduct of the union's business, but safeguarding the power of the leader. Administrative rationality *will* then be maximized at the complete expense of representativeness; and indeed, such things as building up the size of the union (which helps aggrandize the leaders) will be pursued even beyond the point where they threaten efficiency. In other words, representational rationality is entirely deserted; the union no longer does anything to represent its members, and all attempts to try to make it do so will fail. What the critics of Michels are saying is: given that representation is part of the very *raison d'être* of the union, can it be so easily and so irrevocably swept aside?

The critics usually look, quite correctly, for evidence of either successful attacks by members on neglect by leaders or autonomous acts to secure goals by groups within the union which the leader either cannot prevent or simply has to endorse. In both cases a continuing commitment to action within the unions by the members is assumed. But leaders may also be forced to acknowledge the need for good representation by the fact that if they do not, the members will simply leave, depriving the union of the subscriptions and power base which are crucial to what are in Michels's view the central drives of the leaders for status and wealth.[2] In other words, members may simply 'vote with their feet' in Lenin's memorable phrase. This might seem a clear-cut issue, and returns us to the debate over the closed shop. Should we expect to find far stronger oligarchical tendencies in unions, membership of which is a condition of employment? If so, the easiest way to prevent oligarchy among union leaders would be to abolish the closed shop.

But the matter is not so simple. First, we have to ask how the member who leaves the union intends to look after his collective interests. If he is content to belong to no union at all, he has no problem; but a dissatisfied member who wants to belong to a union will find little help in resignation unless he can join an effective alternative. These are not often available. In such a country as Germany, where union rights belong only to particular organizations which are recognized at law, and where a rationalized system of industrial unions exists, there are few opportunities for there being more than one union available to any category of worker.[3] In some countries there are rival unions, but these are often differentiated on religious and political grounds, with, say, separate Catholic, socialist and communist unions; so a decision to change unions may also involve a change of religious faith or political allegiance!

In Britain union structure is very fluid, even chaotic, but there is a firm agreement among unions affiliated to the TUC (the 'Bridlington Agreement') to prevent 'poaching' each other's members. The power of this was shown dramatically in 1969, when workers on strike at the Pilkington Glass Works, St Helens, found they were getting no support from their union, the GMWU. They tried to transfer their membership, *en masse*, to the TGWU, but the TUC intervened under the terms of the Bridlington Agreement to prevent this. In some sectors workers can join one of the unions not affiliated to the TUC in preference to a TUC affiliate, but the latter do their best to ensure that employers do not give such unions bargaining rights, sometimes being willing to strike to prevent recognition of them. On occasions workers dissatisfied with their union have formed 'breakaways' (Lerner, 1961; Hemingway, 1978). Some of these have had lengthy careers, creating considerable trouble for the original union, but they usually encounter the combined strength of existing unions, employers and governmental or other mediatory bodies, none of whom want industrial relations made more complicated or to see new, rival points of strength emerge.

The very care that unions have taken to prevent workers forming or joining rivals may make us suspicious that Michelsian motives are at work, though there is a strong argument to be made from the union side that 'unity is strength', and that a multiplicity of unions will not serve the workers' interests. Nevertheless, this seems a good case for some comparative studies; do union leaderships faced with successful alternatives or breakaways pay more attention to 'representational rationality' than those who are unchallenged? The special case of the closed shop would be a part of such a study. So far no one has attempted such a project.

There is a final twist to this issue which might lessen the significance of 'voting with one's feet' and which throws a new light on the Michels debate. This derives from the argument of Albert Hirschman in his *Exit, Voice and Loyalty* (1970). While working in Nigeria, Hirschman, an economist, noted that although the railways were abysmally inefficient, few people ever complained. On enquiry he found that merchants of any power and importance always sent their goods by the considerably more expensive but efficient road route. Thus the articulate minority was content, and the railways were left to deal with the passive majority who could not afford the road route; so there was no pressure on the railways to improve efficiency, provided they preferred to accept the loss of some business rather than mend their ways. This led Hirschman to speculate further: if for some reason the articulate minority were *forced* to use the railways, they would complain about their inefficiency, and the result could well be an improved transport system for everybody; in other words, it was likely that a perfect monopoly would have produced an overall more efficient service than a situation of limited competition where only the articulate minority was in a position to choose an alternative. This challenged the assumptions of Hirschman's economics training, so he developed a theory of the phenomenon.

'Exit' in the title of his book refers to one's chance of leaving a relationship (say, that of customer of a firm or member of an organization); 'voice' refers to chances to participate in the conduct of the relationship, whether by voting, complaining, sharing in decision-making, lobbying or whatever. Attempts at securing 'loyalty' from customers/members are made by the providers of the goods and services, or leaders of the organization, to try to prevent them choosing to exercise their rights of exit or voice. Hirschman explores various combinations of these categories. The central paradox, illustrated by the Nigerian example, is that elimination of the possibility of exit may render voice more powerful, by forcing the discontented to use their energies to get improvements rather than simply going elsewhere. If those able to go elsewhere are a minority, while the effect of voice activity will be to secure general improvements, there is a net social gain in the use of voice rather than exit techniques.

The theory has widespread practical applications; for example, to the issue of private education or private health care – and perhaps also to that of trade-union membership. If a minority of highly critical members decides to resign from an oligarchical union (exit), leaving a docile mass behind, the leaders will have rid themselves of troublemakers and can settle down to a quiet life; whereas if the critics have to remain members, they may continue to lobby and complain (voice) until the leaders respond or are forced out of office.

This reasoning throws new light on the debate over the closed shop, and makes the idea of research into this question even more interesting. However, for Hirschman's arguments to apply to trade unions, three conditions have to be met: (i) that when critics 'exit', they either have an alternative union available or are content to become non-members; (ii) that in such cases something, if only apathy, can be identified which inhibits the mass of members from deserting the inadequate union; and (iii) that the leaders cannot simply deal with a minority of 'voice' critics by expelling them – a sanction which is of course particularly severe in closed shops.

In conclusion, then, Michels's implicit model of a union in which members are both trapped and incapable of either acting autonomously or of doing anything to arrest the progressive neglect of their representation begs many questions of union structure. At the same time, the fundamental insight that the people charged with running an organization of workers may come to have different interests from those of the members, and that they may be able to ensure that the organization primarily serves their own interests, is of major importance. In addition to the question whether the leaders are *able* to pursue a course of action different from that of the members there is debate over the *direction* that will be taken by this difference. In Michels's own and in subsequent Marxist versions it is always assumed that a treacherous leadership betrays members who were seeking a radical challenge to capitalist oppression. Other accounts also regard the membership (or at least sections of it) as more militant than the leaders, but attribute the difference to the 'statesmanship' and good sense of the leaders, as opposed to the members who take a narrow and ill-informed view. This is often the approach of union leaders themselves and those sympathetic to them. (See, for example, Vic Allen's biography [1957] of Arthur Deakin, one of the most autocratic of British union bosses – a book written, incidentally, before Allen became a Marxist and started to write very different accounts of union leadership.) It is also the view *sometimes* taken by Conservative politicians. But in other circumstances Conservatives are more likely to see an undemocratic, militant and politically motivated leadership forcing ordinary members into radical policies which they do not really want to adopt.[4] A more substantial example of this view was the recent study of a particular union, the Association of Supervisory, Technical and Managerial Staffs, significantly entitled *Reluctant Militants* (Roberts *et al.*, 1972). ASTMS is a particularly striking case: a union with a white-collar, largely managerial membership but one of the most left-wing leaderships in the British union movement. But this view of the militant leaders and the conservative members can also be interpreted differently: as union leaders trying to pursue a far-sighted line which is in the interests of their members, but which some selfish conservatives among the latter are trying to frustrate. This is the accusation made against many breakaway unions by union officials.

Clearly, some of these differences in interpretation of the leader/member division simply reflect the prejudices of the observers. No one has studied systematically the conditions under which unions follow policies at variance with the wishes of their members. Instead, we have individual studies of very different situations – for example, the *Reluctant Militants* study as against the account of the betrayal of workers' interests by co-operation between Labour governments and union leaderships in Panitch's *Social Democracy and Industrial Militancy* (1976). We should beware of attempts at drawing generalizations from these studies of varying unions, varying issues and varying moments of time. To take a specific example, it is entirely possible that in winter 1979 many ordinary lorry drivers and local-authority employees did want to press radical pay claims while some of their leaders wanted to restrain them out of loyalty to the Labour government; and that by 1981 these same workers so feared unemployment that they did not want to risk big pay claims, while some union leaders believed that the government's bluff could be called. And on both occasions there were both workers and union leaders who took the opposite line to the majority of their peers.

In retrospect it seems that, in line with Michelsian expectations, most union leaders were taken by surprise by the shop-floor resurgence of the late 1960s, and that several of them regretted that it had occurred; that resurgence certainly caused them problems in their relations with the Labour government. But it is also the case that most unions took steps to give more power to recognized shop-floor

groups within their decision-making and negotiating structures – though again it could be argued that their motive
here was to tame the unofficial movement by incorporating
it. Then, again, unions and shop stewards were slow in
responding to the apparent change in mood away from
militancy in the early 1980s; this is difficult to explain with
Michelsian assumptions. After some cases of workers' refusal to support strike calls, several unions began to make
increasing use of ballots, where before leaders or stewards
might have relied upon their own judgement; a sign
that officials have lost confidence in their ability either
to interpret the mood of their members or to give them
instructions with a presumption that they will be followed. In other words, it is not easy to fit the twists
and turns of recent British union history into any one of the
stereotyped accounts of relations between officials and
members.

An alternative to Michels

While it would be instructive to see an extended comparative study of problems of intra-union relations under varying conditions, most progress can be made by abandoning
the search for systematic differences between leader and
member positions on the 'militancy/conservatism' axis and
looking instead for a different kind of division that might
more accurately reflect their different positions in relation
to union business.

In the last chapter we distinguished between two types
of goal: substantive goals which materially improved
workers' living and working standards; and procedural
goals, for control over or a share in control over different
aspects of the capital-labour relationship. In this chapter I
shall refer to these as money goals and participation goals
respectively: money goals, because however varied the different substantive goals, they have in common the fact that

they all increase the cost of labour, and can all be expressed in money terms. I use participation rather than control, because the former is a wider term, referring to a broader range of possibilities – 'control' referring to the extreme case of decision-making by workers alone. It might be argued that participation goals can also be reduced to money terms, in that they 'cost' the efficiency forgone by allowing workers to dilute managerial control. But it is highly contentious whether participation does reduce efficiency; it is sometimes argued that it actually increases it, or at least that it is indifferent to it. The contention that it necessarily reduces efficiency is a part of managerial ideology which cannot be assumed to be true at the level of theory.

The reason for re-introducing this distinction between two sorts of goals is that union members and leaders (or officers) stand in a contrasting relationship to them. Money gains are received and enjoyed by individual workers and in most cases they exercise individual choice over the consumption of the gains: the individual worker spends (or saves) a pay increase, enjoys the increased leisure afforded by reduced working hours, benefits from safer working conditions. The union leadership receives no direct money gains itself from bargaining activity, but it does have an indirect interest in the success of its own part in bargaining activity, because its hold on members' loyalty depends on it. The leadership, as an organization, *does* gain directly from pursuing participation goals, for these activities extend its role and scope: it is the actor within certain kinds of participation activity, such as collective bargaining, membership of government committees, sharing in decision-making. It is not so much the purposes to which participation can be put as the *fact* of having it which is a goal for the organization; it is the act of participating which enhances its standing, fulfils its *raison d'être*. The members may eventually gain from the union's participation activities, but this will be a doubly indirect benefit. It is indirect, first because the participation is carried out at the remote level of the national leadership, being (except in special cases) out of reach of the members' immediate influence; and, second, because the fact of participation does not itself guarantee favourable outcomes. One implication of this is the potentiality for conflicting interests in bargaining between leaders and members. The union's central interest is in securing its capacity to make deals; while the members' interest is in the substantive outcome. The union will therefore take steps to secure the unity and strength of the membership (under its control), to maintain the stability of the bargaining relationship, and to guarantee its own capacity to 'deliver' its side of any agreement (in order to establish its credibility as a bargaining partner). These are all activities which may lead it to restrain members' immediate pursuit of material gains.

As Pizzorno (1978: 284) has pointed out in an analysis of this difference of positions, the scope for conflict and distrust between members and union is intensified by the different time horizons implied by the distinction between participation (or power) and money goals:

... power means, or should mean, capacity to obtain benefits in the future. So, when the organization which represents the workers becomes more powerful – by receiving new positions of power instead of immediate benefits for its members – it is by this token strengthening its capacity for obtaining future benefits. But the possibility of a gap between the interest of the represented and the interests of the representative exists in the sacrifice of immediate benefits for the sake of future gains, when the union has the monopoly of legitimate interpretation of what is best, of what constitutes the 'true', that is long-term, interests of its members. In choosing power rather than immediate gains, it acquires positions which allow it more freedom of interpretation. The power of obtaining future benefits then becomes power over its own members.

So far we have treated the leadership as a unified, central whole. This is unrealistic. In practice there may be different factions within a leadership; and there are different levels of officers (national, regional, local, etc.); and different types of officers, ranging from elected leaders to appointed administrative officials. But to avoid being overwhelmed by all these possible variations, it is necessary when building theory to proceed step by step, adding more variables at each point in order to bring our model a little nearer realistic situations. For the present discussion we shall explore just one variation in the concept of union leadership, but one of crucial practical importance: the distinction between national and shop-floor leadership, the latter meaning, in British industrial relations, primarily shop stewards, or sometimes entirely unofficial leading activists.

Relations between a shop-floor leadership and the members are different from those between national leaders and members. First, there are not the same problems of remoteness between the organization and the membership; the participants in the organization are themselves workers, and the members have more immediate access to and influence over them than they do with respect to the national leadership. Second, the Olsonian problems of collective action will not be so serious at plant level, so there is not the same gulf between a passive membership and an apparatus erected to do the collective task for them. Finally, the participation goals which may be pursued locally are different from those at national level, and may involve more direct involvement by the workers themselves.

Figure 5.1 indicates the range of different interests at stake in the positions of individual workers, shop-floor organizations and national union leaderships. The two kinds of goals (money and participation) have each been subdivided into those aspects which can be pursued at the two different levels being considered. The strength of interest in the different goals by different actors is represented by numbers (which are used purely ordinally). An immediate, direct interest, that is, a strong interest for the actor concerned, is denoted by a 3. An indirect interest is denoted by a 2; while 1 denotes a weak, that is, a doubly indirect interest.

Figure 5.1 Interests of different labour actors in different kinds of goals

Goals	Actors		
	Individual workers	*Shop–floor organization*	*National union leadership*
Money: shop–level	3	2–3	1
Money: national level	3	1	2–3
Participation: shop–level	2	3	1
Participation: national level	1	1	3

Individual workers have a strong interest in money goals from whatever source, because they are the direct recipients of any gains. Their interest in shop-level participation is less direct, because it is their *representatives* who actually participate. However, these are representatives to whom they have direct access and who can be expected to be responsive to shop-floor concerns. Individual workers have, as already discussed, only a doubly indirect interest in national-level participation goals.

The shop-floor organization, that is, the shop stewards and those closely associated with them, has an interest in plant-level money goals ranging from strong to medium strong. It is an indirect interest in that the organization as organization does not benefit directly from wage gains, but it will gain prestige and standing among the workforce if it can secure such gains for them. The strength of this interest will therefore depend on the extent to which the organization needs continuous reinforcement of its standing among the members. The interest of the shop-floor organization in national-level money goals is weak; not only does it not gain from this activity itself, but it is carried on without its involvement. Indeed, the shop-floor organization may occasionally have a *negative* interest in success at this level, because the more that is gained nationally, the less remains for it to achieve. The interest of the shop-floor organization in shop-level participation goals is of course very high, while its interest in national-level participation is low for the same reason as for national money goals.

Where both kinds of goal are concerned, the national leadership has preferences which are the reverse of those of the shop-floor organization, for obvious reasons.[5] If anything, the chances of the leadership having a strong interest in money goals secured at its own level are somewhat less than those of the shop-floor organization, because national leaderships will usually be less dependent on day-to-day support from the members.

This account of differing interests shares the consensus among many observers of unions that there are differences of interest between different levels of the union movement, but it differs from them in not needing to make moral judgements as the means of defining the differences. It is not a question of 'irresponsible' shop stewards, or of leaders who 'sell out' the membership, but of different structural positions in the system of representation leading to differences, sometimes conflicts, of interest – even though all the interests can be seen as serving the ends of improving the standard of living of workers.

Examples of the conflicts implied by the account are easy to find. For example, in 1979 the management of British Leyland offered its workforce a major wage increase on condition that the workers surrendered the mass of local bargaining arrangements that had developed in the company and accepted centralized bargaining. The shop stewards at the company opposed the plan: the achievements of local bargaining had been won by their struggles, and it was they who represented workers' interests within them; abolition of local bargaining would considerably weaken the importance of the shop stewards' organization within the company. The management appealed over the stewards' heads to the workers at large, who in a secret ballot in 1980 accepted the management's offer: the local bargaining structure was only an indirect interest for them, whereas the wage increases were something they would receive as individuals.

This does not mean that workers will always choose to relinquish controls in exchange for cash if given the chance; much will depend on the size of the cash offer and the importance to the workers of their indirect interest in controls. Relevant factors in the Leyland case were that the company was facing severe economic difficulties, the workers fearing that there was little scope left for constant gains through local bargaining, while some shop-floor groups had so frequently used the opportunities for strikes afforded by decentralization that many workers were fed up with constant disruption and loss of pay.

Figure 5.2 'Rates of exchange' between money goals and various types of participation goals

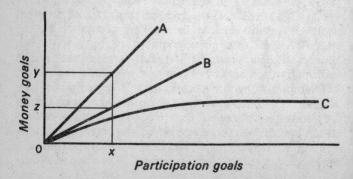

To understand the problem facing workers here we can return to the analysis in chapter 4 of workers' choice between different goals, adding this new element of the indirectness of the workers' interest in many participation goals. In figure 5.2 the line OA represents a supposed 'rate of exchange' that we assume workers subjectively establish between units of control or participation and units of pay increase, on the assumption that the participation is exercised by them as individuals. If the employer wants to regain x units of control, he has to offer £y. Now, let us assume that the participation is exercised, not by the workers, but by a collectivity, a shop stewards' organization or elected representatives. This renders the control or participation goal indirect and hence devalues it, worsening its rate of exchange against pay rises as shown in OB. To win back his x units of control the employer now needs to offer only £z. However, it will be no use his trying to win more than x units for that sum, or to pay less than £z for x units, because indirect though the gains are, they are still positively evaluated. Two factors therefore determine the workers' rate of exchange between money and control: (i) their preference between money and participation goals *per se* (measured by the slope of OA), which will be affected by their need for more money relative to their need to control their work; and (ii) the degree of their alienation from the collectivity which exercises control (measured by the angle between OA and OB), which will depend on the means by which the participation is exercised and the attitude of the workers to the relevant shop stewards' group or other organization.

If we further assume – as will be partly true – that successive increases in worker-participation involve moving further away from the shop floor, then we find that, at each level of control increase, the problem of indirectness *worsens*. Rather than remaining proportional to the original rate of exchange, as in the straight line OB, it will be a curve, as in OC, which may eventually become a straight line; that is, after a certain point the level at which participation is exercised will be so remote from the workers that they will be indifferent to it. Workers will be more willing to exchange these controls for relatively small sums or, to look at the same relationship differently, they will be less inclined to sacrifice pay demands in order to pursue these participation objectives.

Returning to figure 5.1, there is a further interesting contrast between the three different social actors identified. The two most strongly contrasted positions are those of the national leadership and the shop-floor organization; the individual workers stand in between them. It is not the case that the pattern of interests moves from individual workers, through shop-floor organization to the national leadership, as one might expect. This is because the workers' prime concern is with the receipt of substantive goals from whatever source, while the two organizations have their interests concentrated on securing participation at their respective, and sometimes conflicting, levels. While there is scope for conflict between workers and the national leadership, and between workers and the shop-floor leadership, it is likely that the biggest conflicts between different levels of the labour movement will be between national and local organizations, with the workers left in the middle, somewhat *hors de combat*. The recent refutations of the Michelsian 'iron law' have mainly stressed the capacity for resistance against national leaders of shop-floor *activists*, organized groups. The literature has tended to regard these groups as synonymous with the membership *as a whole*, but this is not necessarily the case.

National leaderships have always been very suspicious of the tendency for local organizations to assume an autonomous existence, dependent on them though they are for the union's strength at the workplace. This is often because the shop-floor groups are likely to break bargains made by the national leadership in order to gain local improvements. National leaders' objections to this are often regarded as evidence of their incorporation by employers, but this is not necessarily so. They may simply be looking after their own interests as the national organization. If the national leadership wants to safeguard participation rights at its own level, it has to be able to keep the bargains it makes; an employer will not be impressed by a demand to reach an agreement if he knows the agreement will not be honoured for long by the workers' side. Union officers must therefore be expected to try to prevent shop-floor groups breaking the agreements it has made on the workers' behalf. For their part, the shop-floor groups cannot be expected to place as much priority on the needs of the national leadership as they do on their own need to secure participation rights.

Evidence of central-local tensions
National leaderships have harried and hindered the development of shop-floor organizations at many points. The first shop stewards' movement during the First World War was indeed launched in the face of national leaders' co-operation with the government, so national-local relations were particularly fraught (Hinton, 1973). During the second great period of growth in shop-floor movements, from the 1950s on, union leaders did not so much oppose the development outright as try to contain it; after all, the original function of shop stewards was to act as dues collectors for the unions. Provided they kept their activities to the individual shop, the national unions raised little objection. They did, however, oppose most strongly attempts to develop shop stewards' combine committees running across several firms in a district, or several plants in a company; once the shop-floor organization started to do that, it was trespassing on territory which the national leadership regarded as its own (Lerner and Bescoby, 1966).

By the 1970s the situation had changed a little. Many unions had, following the developments of the late 1960s, taken steps to formalize shop stewards' role within the union. At the same time the great wave of company mergers which had been affecting British capitalism since the mid-

1960s made inter-plant co-operation among workers within individual giant companies an urgent matter. At a firm like the Ford Motor Company joint shop stewards' committees representing several unions and all the company's plants met regularly and formulated the main annual wage claim with the full co-operation of most union leaderships. More generally, several unions took steps to decentralize their organization and decision-making, providing shop-floor groups with a formal union role. By the early 1970s even a union as centralized as the GMWU was rapidly developing a shop-floor movement, and by the end of the decade such traditionally weakly organized and highly centralized groups as local government manual staff were equipped with shop-floor organization. This development considerably eased tension between leaderships and local activists, though in a way which caused new problems for both when the national officers became involved in agreements over income restraint in the Social Contract with the 1974–9 Labour government; but that is part of the story of the next chapter.

It was during the late 1950s, as shop-floor movements spread, that observers began to take an interest in the distinction between strikes called by national leaders and those called by local groups – the difference between 'official' and 'unofficial' strikes. Strictly speaking, people were more interested in the difference between 'constitutional' and 'unconstitutional' strikes: that between strikes called in accordance with agreed procedure and those called against the procedural rules. In practice the two classifications overlap heavily: official unions rarely strike in breach of agreement, because they are usually the agents in a procedure agreement, while shop-floor groups often do. However, it is the name 'unofficial' strike which has stuck. Since 1961 the Ministry of Labour (now called the Department of Employment) has produced statistics on the proportion of strikes known to be unofficial. The proportion varies from year to year, but has so far stayed within a range of 93 to 98 per cent (see table 5.1). In other words, nearly all strikes are unofficial; a strike called by an official union is a rarity. This is partly because the local scale of shop-floor action means that there are far more points at which a strike can be decided than within the smaller number of national union leaderships; if one looks at the proportion of days lost in strikes which are unofficial, or the proportion of workers on strike who are on unofficial strike, the figures look very different, as can be seen from table 5.1. However, the reason for the disparity is also that so many more issues appear which can be dealt with quickly by strike action at local level than can at national level,

Table 5.1 Proportion of strike activity which is unofficial (%)

Year	Number of strikes	Workers involved	Days lost
1962	96·8	13·8	29·1
1963	97·6	86·4	70·0
1964	97·2	81·5	69·7
1965	95·9	89·2	79·2
1966	96·9	90·6	51·1
1967	94·9	95·1	85·9
1968	96·2	30·6	53·1
1969	96·9	82·9	76·4
1970	95·9	83·5	69·8
1971	92·8	67·9	25·8
1972	93·6	63·1	23·8
1973	95·4	73·8	72·1
1974	95·7	71·2	52·3
1975	93·9	89·9	80·9
1976	96·6	93·1	85·6
1977	97·1	82·2	75·2
1978	96·4	87·7	56·9
1979	96·1	20·4	20·2
1980	95·0	51·3	15·7

Source: *Department of Employment Gazette*

when a ponderous procedure has to be used in order to get action taken.

Because of the tension between national and local leaderships it might be assumed that unofficial strikes are strikes 'against' the national leadership as much as against the employer, and some observers have seen it as precisely that, the most outstanding example being the major international study of industrial conflict produced during the 1950s (Ross and Hartmann, 1960). This recorded the sharp decline that was taking place in strike activity virtually throughout the Western world, with the exception of the United States and Canada. Many (perhaps, as was certainly the case in Britain, most) of the remaining strikes were unofficial. This meant, argued the authors, that conflict between workers and employers, or between unions and employers, had virtually ceased; unofficial strikes were strikes by workers against union *leaderships*. They argued this on the grounds that these strikes were in breach of agreements negotiated and therefore approved by the leaders.

This was inaccurate. While *some* unofficial strikes are 'anti-official', in that union officials actively oppose them and regard them as a rejection of the deals they have secured for the members, others are simply 'a-official', in the sense that the existence of the union and its procedures and signed agreements are simply not relevant. If the workers in the paint shop of an automotive plant decide that the air-conditioning is not adequate to remove the paint fumes, they will walk off the job in order to force the management to do something about it, probably without a thought of what the union might think or do about it. Indeed, such strikes may not always be unconstitutional (i.e., in breach of an agreement), because they may concern a question not covered in any agreements, whether procedural or substantive. On other occasions the union may be well aware of the strike and indeed be in contact with the strikers, with all concerned being content that the dispute continue as an unofficial one; for various reasons neither strikers nor officials may want to have the union officially involved.

Another reason for not taking too seriously the official/unofficial distinction is that unions differ considerably in the rules by which they deem a strike official. For example, in the National Union of Mineworkers an official strike can take place only after approval by a ballot of the membership. Clearly, such a slow and cumbersome procedure is of little use in the case of sudden local disputes, so all strikes in mining except very rare, national wage disputes are unofficial. In other unions the decision to recognize a strike, which often brings with it the decision to offer strike pay, can be taken by national or regional officers. At the other extreme from the NUM comes ASTMS, the officers of which are often willing to give *retrospective* recognition to an unofficial dispute started by some of their members. Indeed, it is by no means unusual for strikes which start life as unofficial to end as official disputes of the union.

The tension between levels of organization should not be exaggerated. The fact that such tension does exist, that union organizations are not merely the reflection of their members' wishes, has to be discussed at length because the opposite assumption is so unrealistic. But probably the most typical form of relationship between shop-floor groups and at least the local level of the union bureaucracy is one of interdependence. The office needs the work of the shop stewards and other activists in recruiting people to the union, keeping them loyal to it and providing its basic means of mobilization. But the shop-floor organization also needs the advice and assistance of the union. It is important to understand this, or one may wonder why powerful shop-floor organizations bother to stay affiliated to a national union at all.[6] This question was considered by Batstone *et al.* (1977) in their study of shop stewards' organizations. They considered the evidence for and against (i) a 'maturity thesis', that is, that as they mature, so shop-floor or 'domestic' organizations become quite autonomous from the larger national union, and (ii) a 'cycle of dependence' theory which argues that, as full 'maturity' is reached, so certain countervailing factors are set in motion which swing the domestic organization back to dependence on the larger union, and so on. They conclude that the latter theory fits the facts better:

> Such an idea is based upon the fact that domestic organizations are themselves not automatically unified entities. The cycle of dependence rests upon the view, that as one level of organization achieves power and an institutionalized position, subordinate groups will begin to challenge it. The domestic organization may achieve a degree of independence from the larger union, and this will result in a concentration of power in the hands of the convenors. In this situation, other stewards develop an awareness of their own power and attempt to exert it in opposition to the convenors and in pursuit of their own sectional interests. This may well occur because of increasing wage differentials, themselves the product of action by the domestic organization. The declining unity of the organization fosters a new dependence upon the larger union, this being encouraged by members of the organization itself, full-time officials, and by management. [p. 216]

This may seem a little mechanistic, and there may be other factors which also help maintain the link with the larger union: the very *idea* of a national trade-union movement, which will be important to stewards and activists if not to many ordinary members; the value of the union's legal and other advisory services; the fact that even the most independent convenors of shop stewards would feel alone in a hostile world if they did not have some link with a wider, national organization with resources and a reputation behind it. It is certainly remarkable, though rarely commented on, that during the 1960s and 1970s, when the autonomy of domestic organizations reached an all-time peak in this country, and when, from time to time, the pressures from unions' national offices to persuade their members to accept restraint were also at a peak, there was no move at all to establish a network of local, autonomous, shop-steward-level bodies that were not affiliated to national unions. Indeed, these were years of union amalgamation; and the movement that did take place was towards the integration of shop-floor activity within the national unions.

6 The Inevitability of Politics

British trade unions, like those of nearly all other countries, are deeply involved in politics. In this country they founded the Labour Party and remain today its main paymasters and by far the biggest voting strength at its annual conference; whatever political party is in office, they have dealings with it and offer it advice on a range of policy issues; and on several occasions in the past three decades they have become involved in agreements with governments over wage restraint. On the other hand, opinion polls report widespread dissatisfaction among union members with unions playing any political role at all, a view shared by Conservative politicians, newspapers, and many employers. More strangely, there is considerable evidence that unions themselves do not take their wider political role very seriously. A fact commonly noted is that, while the major union leaders ensure that they themselves sit on the General Council of the TUC, they send a lower level of official to represent their unions on the National Executive Committee of the Labour Party.

A recent study of political involvement by the two largest British unions, the TGWU and the Amalgamated Union of Engineering Workers, concluded that:

... the underlying objective of [union] political action in the post-war years was simply the achievement, maintenance or restoration of 'free collective bargaining'. Whenever there is a threat to the legal status of unionism or to free collective bargaining, trade unionism moves towards genuine political action to counter that threat. [Richter, 1973: 218]

But when union rights were secure and collective bargaining unrestrained, unions had very few political goals. In other words, the purpose of unions' political action is simply to ensure the non-interference of politics in their industrial activity. Richter argues that this was true of the early history of Labour politics, including the original decision of the unions to sponsor a political party; and of the role of union leaders even during the period of the first post-war Labour government. He saw no divergence from this pattern in the new politicization of British unions which began in the late 1960s:

> ... in 1967 the TUC began to utilize its political power to resist statutory incomes policies, and by 1969–71, for the first time since World War II, the British unions were committed to serious rather than spurious political action. However, the purpose was essentially the same as it had been in 1900–06 – to restore 'free' collective bargaining. This shows definitely the limits within which one may expect trade union political action to function, unless and until the unions awaken to the imperatives of the managed economy, or decide to move towards other social alternatives. [*ibid*: 245]

The author, an American, was working in an important tradition of US trade-union theory founded by Selig Perlman (1928), who claimed that whatever political issues might feature in their rhetoric, trade unions were essentially interested only in what he called 'pure and simple unionism', the search for higher pay for their members. In the words of Samuel Gompers, leader of the first American union confederation (the American Federation of Labor) in the early twentieth century, defining union goals with an elegant simplicity not at all achieved in chapter 4 of this volume: 'What we want is – MORE!'

American unions are notable among the labour movements of the world for their lack of involvement in politics – though they do provide an important arm of support for the Democratic Party, especially in the north-eastern states – and perhaps Richter was seeing British unions through jaundiced American eyes. However, a recent study of the

Union of Post-Office Workers[1] by a British political scientist (Moran, 1974) describes the marginal status of political activity in an important British union, the leaders of which are often involved in political actions. While he found uniformed staffs (e.g., postmen) more willing to support militancy and political action than the non-uniformed (e.g., post-office counter clerks, telephone exchange operators), even 'most uniformed workers are still characterized by a highly calculative outlook, think the union should concern itself solely with economic objectives, are opposed to affiliation with a political party and do not support the idea of a closed shop' (p. 57). Contrary to the author's initial expectations, this lack of sympathy among the mass of members with the political activity of the union did not reduce the UPW's effectiveness, and the great majority of the members interviewed reported their satisfaction with the union. The answer, he suggests, lay in their widespread ignorance of what the union actually did in its wider political work, and the massive apathy which made the members content to leave such matters to a minority of activists (*ibid*: 147–8).

There is an important paradox here. Unions are involved in a major way in a very significant activity – the political life of the country – and yet there is considerable evidence that they do not take that activity very seriously. We could explain this by regarding the unions' political role as an historical accident; after all, as Richter points out, British unions only took an interest in forming the Labour Party after they had suffered from an adverse legal judgement in the Taff Vale Railway case of 1901,[2] and their political aims were then largely limited to putting pressure on governments to change the law affecting their bargaining activities. They gave little thought to the possibility that the Labour Party might eventually replace the Liberals as one of the two great parties in the state, often being in government office. What if the Taff Vale case had never occurred? Would the unions never have entered politics? Is the unions' party involvement now merely kept going by a few politically ambitious men, who use the union machinery and take advantage of their members' apathy, in order to strut around the political stage with no real base behind them?

But there are other ways of regarding the issue. It is notable that a union political affiliation is not a British oddity, as the above account of the importance of the Taff Vale case might suggest; if one includes the American unions' rather fragile relationship with the Democratic Party, there are no important trade-union confederations in the industrial world which do not have significant links with a political party. These links are not always formal; indeed, though many British unions are affiliated to the Labour Party, the TUC itself is not. But there is often a pattern of interlocking personnel – union leaders becoming ministers, for example, as occurs in many countries; representation of unions on the governing bodies of the party, as happens in the British and Australian Labour Parties and in the French Communist Party; collaboration over election programmes, financial support for parties, as well as a mass of overlapping personnel among the activists of party and union.

If Britain is odd, it is in the direction of original parentage:[3] the British unions founded the Labour Party; elsewhere, socialist parties forged trade-union movements out of the congeries of craft societies that were emerging with industrialism. To take an extreme case, for several years in the 1890s the Swedish Social Democratic and Labour Party *was* the trade-union confederation.

There are in all countries unions, usually of white-collar or professional workers, with no political affiliation; and in some cases, such as the French Force Ouvrière, there are small confederations which try to stand outside politics. But the universal norm is of close connections with a political party, mainly a Labour or Communist Party, but often with right-of-centre religious-based parties, usually but not always of Roman Catholic origin.

Is political involvement by unions an important aspect

of their activity or not? Using our rational-choice approach, we must ask under what conditions may unions most effectively pursue their goals, and is political action relevant to the achievement of them? If the answer to the latter is affirmative, we must ask how the choices confronting union actors might nevertheless lead them to regard this political action as unimportant. Historically, the explanation of union political involvement is concerned with the achievement of basic legal rights to organize or, more generally, with the struggle for universal suffrage and working-class political rights. But to leave the explanation there implies that we are today left with a mere anachronism. We need to explore whether we can derive the idea of political action from the logic of trade unions' everyday *economic* activity. To the extent that we can, we may be confident that we are dealing with something substantial and deeply rooted. We must therefore temporarily leave discussion of politics *per se* and return to the industrial context with which we have been preoccupied in earlier chapters.

The problem of strategic choice

As we have noted at several points, pursuit of a money goal must at some point bring a choice between higher wages (or equivalent gains) and employment. Unions are likely to pursue higher wages at the risk of unemployment, because it is usually only people in work who have a chance to affect union policy. Once a worker is unemployed, there is little that a union can do to represent him. However, unemployment weakens unions; the strike threat is ineffective if there are plenty of unemployed workers to take strikers' places, and union activists are vulnerable to dismissal when they can easily be replaced. Workers and unions are therefore caught in some genuine dilemmas by the wage/employment conflict.

In practice, several factors soften the dilemma. Unionized workers may be able to make their money gains purely at the expense of unorganized groups: the low paid, women workers, immigrants, white-collar workers. Alternatively, wage gains may be made at the expense of profits. This is of course the case which looms largest in union rhetoric. Its practical importance is somewhat less. First, it applies strictly only to the private sector – unless public-sector workers can somehow ensure that their rises are financed from taxation levied primarily on profits, an unlikely position. Second, 'profits' are not equivalent to capitalist earnings. Profits are also the source of new investment, on which future employment probably depends, so wage increases at the expense of profits may frequently turn out not to be a way out of the wage/employment dilemma after all. However, it may be a solution for individual groups of workers, in that the jobs lost as a result of a cut in investment may not be the jobs of the workers who secured the wage increase.

More promising for unions is the scope for creaming off excess profits in monopolistic and oligopolistic sectors of the economy – a very high proportion of a modern industrial economy, especially when one adds the entire public sector, including nationalized industries. This is because by definition these concerns earn surplus profits. By organizing, labour is able to take a share of these (Sylos-Labini, 1976). The argument is made formally by Burkitt (1975), who discusses the position of the monopolist in the product market as a *monopsonist* in the labour market. Following the usual logic of monopsony theory, he shows that such an employer will:

increase profits by reducing labour costs through cutting back employment. The lack of reserves and the insecurity of individual wage earners will mean that many are prepared to work at a lower wage level, and the monopsonist can maintain low wages by not extending employment to the higher wage group.

Trade unions can cure this situation by making the wage demands of all workers uniform – at a higher level. This is one of the purposes of the 'common rule' ... which fixes one wage offer for the entire membership. At any wage-rate below the union offer, the supply of labour available to the employer can be reduced to zero by strike action. Thus, in so far as the workforce supports union policy, the union creates a perfectly elastic labour supply at the official rate, and the monopsonist is no longer able to reduce wages by reducing the number of workers he employs. [p. 16]

If, instead, the employer tries to pay higher wages to attract marginal workers while keeping his existing workforce on lower pay, the union can again respond by demanding the common rate for the job.

Even in competitive situations, unions may be able to achieve real wage gains without threatening employment levels. Assuming demand remains high, an employer wanting to replace labour which has become expensive will install new plant and equipment of lower labour intensity. But that takes time, so in the short term he has to go on employing labour (*ibid*: 32). Meanwhile, in the long term, if workers' wages continue to rise across the economy, demand for goods will be increased (including the demand for capital goods among employers replacing expensive labour). To the extent that this demand is satisfied on the home market, there will be an increase in the demand for labour despite the replacement of labour taking place through the increase in capital intensity.

However, such processes cannot continue indefinitely, nor will they operate under all circumstances. What if the effect of a wage increase on prices leads to a reduction in demand? What if domestically produced goods become so expensive that workers spend their higher incomes on imported goods and capitalists buy their new capital equipment from overseas? What if, even in the oligopolistic sector, wage rises so reduce capitalists' profits that the latter reduce investment in order to protect their own consumption standards or to invest in more profitable sectors or countries? The effect of all these conditions will be to reduce employment. A union strategy of constantly increasing wages (or labour costs in general) is only compatible with continuing high employment levels under certain macro-economic conditions; and these conditions are themselves beyond the reach of collective bargaining activity.

There is a further problem. If we assume that most workers in an economy are successfully achieving wage rises as a result of union bargaining, and if we further assume that at least in the short run demand remains sufficiently high in the economy for employers to be able to raise prices to pay for these wage rises, we have a familiar situation: inflation, or a general rise in the price level. The effect of inflation, of course, is to erode the value of a rise in incomes. If wages rise by 20 per cent but prices rise by 18 per cent, then real wages have risen by only 2 per cent. The wage bargainer, the union official or shop steward, can still claim to his members that he has achieved a 20 per cent wage increase, but that is not what the members experience in practice. Whether or not they perceive any link between the activities of union wage bargainers and that rise of 18 per cent in the price level will be a factor affecting relations between unions and their members. Gaining a pay rise by means of a price rise is a self-defeating activity when viewed from a macro-economic perspective, though for a particular work-group their individual wage rise may seem very remote from the combined effects of many such work-groups on the overall price level.

Of course, not all groups suffer equally from the effects of inflation, and some work-groups may have enough strength to keep their wages rising faster than the price level. But even this cannot continue indefinitely. Inflation damages business confidence, which leads to a decline in investment and hence in employment; in fact, governments are likely to act during the early stages of an inflation to reduce any general collapse of confidence by taking steps to reduce demand. This will probably reduce inflation, but at the expense of, again, reducing employment.

There are, therefore, distinct limits on what can be

achieved by trade unions in improving the wages and conditions of their members by action bounded by the market economy, that is, by free collective bargaining. The politico-economic conditions under which this has occurred are well summarized by Burkitt (p. 149):

The situation in which trade unions play an important role in generating inflation yet are unable substantially to redistribute income in favour of wages and away from profits, arises because a changed social and economic environment has enabled the union movement to secure sufficient power to disturb the smooth operation of the capitalist system while possessing insufficient strength to achieve fundamental changes in its social ethos and power structure.

Eventually, organized labour must bump its head against the wage/employment constraint. A very important point, following our discussion of different levels of union decision-making in the previous chapter, is that that constraint presses much harder against a national leadership than against decentralized shop-floor groups. This can be illustrated if we consider the choices presented to two different labour actors by the different possibilities for absorbing pay rises discussed above. First, let us take the extreme case of a trade-union confederation which decides wage bargaining policy for labour across a whole country; this is not entirely unrealistic, since it corresponds broadly to the situation which exists in Sweden, Norway and Austria. Second, let us take the case of a shop-floor group, perhaps organized by a shop stewards' committee, bargaining for workers within part of a large corporation, a common situation in British industry during the 1960s and 1970s. Both labour actors will be willing to take gains from the unorganized sector, since by definition both are concerned only with the interests of organized labour. However, there is far more scope for making gains at the expense of other *unionized* groups for the decentralized unit; all they need worry about is the interests of their own work-group. The centralized confederation, in contrast, has to be concerned with the position of all organized labour; there is no point in its securing an advance for one of its constituent groups at the expense of another – unless, that is, the former group is far more important within the structure and politics of the union movement. Typically, centralized union movements aim at what is known as 'solidaristic' wages policy:[4] ensuring that different groups of the working class do not stray too far out of line from each other, and probably trying to secure higher rates of increase for the lower paid. The strategy of a British shop-floor group is the direct opposite of that, thriving on the scope for 'leap-frogging'. (For an extended version of this argument and an analysis of a number of countries, see Crouch, forthcoming.)

There is also more scope for the shop-floor group in any chances of taking gains at the expense of profits. The horizons of a shop-floor organization are limited to developments predictably affecting their own group; if they took an interest in wider macro-economic effects, they would not normally have the resources for securing information on them; and even if they did, it would never be predictable how a macro-economic development would affect them in particular. The position of the centralized labour actor is very different. Its decisions will affect pay, and therefore profits, across a whole country; it cannot therefore ignore the effects which this may have on investment throughout the economy, because almost inevitably the employment of some of its members somewhere will be affected.

The same logic works for wage rises and inflation. For the small group, the effect of its particular wage rise on the overall level of prices in the economy which its members will eventually have to face as consumers is infinitesimally small; in no way can it be expected to worry about it. Indeed, if the group foresees a rise in the general price level as likely, it is its duty to ensure that it puts in a very high wage claim, or its members will lose out. The group that says it will restrain its wage claim in order to help combat inflation will simply be overwhelmed by the inflation caused by everyone else, while its own abstention will make no impact at all on the overall price level. In contrast, again, the centralized labour actor knows that its decision to press for a particular wage rise across the board will have an inflationary effect (i) from which all its members will then suffer and (ii) which it can appreciably reduce by conscious wage restraint.

As this last case makes clear, union wage behaviour, especially in an inflationary context, is a good case of the logic of collective action. Small-group actors are in a mass situation; the actions of any one actor have a minute effect on the whole, while the cost borne by any one actor which decides alone to follow the collective interest (wage restraint) is severe. As a result, each group follows the logic of its individual interest, and the collective goal in avoiding inflation is incapable of being pursued. The centralized labour actor is not in a mass position; the individual actor is capable of affecting the whole system and of benefiting from the consequences. It is therefore capable of acting in the collective interest. Olson (1978) has pursued this argument in the related context of the impact on economic growth of the organization of interests – of which trade unions are, of course, a prime example.

Back to politics

But within what framework does the centralized labour actor operate? So far in discussing unions and workers we have talked about action contained within the economy, confined to relations with employers, or capital. A labour actor operating at the level of the entire economy is moving in the field of a very important third party in labour relations: the state. Conversely, a state responsible for overall economic management and confronted by a decentralized labour movement trapped in the logic of collective action might try to fashion a centralized collective labour actor. At this point, therefore, we have entered the domain of politics, and demonstrated the near-inevitable drift of trade-union behaviour into politics, whether its members like it or not and whether its leaders take much interest in it or not.

Near-inevitable? Why not inevitable? First, a labour movement may fail to achieve any degree of centralization at all, and remain just an array of local groups, never confronting macro-economic issues at any level of action. This was the case in the early days of trade unionism, but it is a remarkable fact that in every advanced capitalist society unions have eventually come together to form a limited number of confederations; and also that those unions which have nothing to do with politics are usually outside confederations, or are members of very small ones.

Second, a union, or confederation of unions, may be limited in its membership to workers with secure labour-market positions who need not bother much about problems of *general* labour costs. The prime examples of this are confederations of white-collar workers, who, significantly, are rarely involved in politics. This factor may also partly explain the relative political abstention of labour unions in the USA, where unionization tends to be limited to economically secure groups.

Finally, a government may so run its economic policy that it allows excessive labour costs to be translated into unemployment with neither any concern for union complaints about unemployment, nor any desire on its own part to gain union agreement to wage restraint in order to keep unemployment down. In such a situation the unions may well be highly political, in their protests against a state policy of allowing high unemployment, but they will not be drawn into the network of co-operation with government and employers to try to secure restraint over labour costs. Something of this has often characterized US economic policy; it was the case in many countries in the 1920s and 1930s; and it is largely true of British government policy since the election of the Conservatives to office in 1979.

Outside these exceptions it may be assumed that the

national centres of trade-union movements, and probably
individual unions, will become drawn into questions of
macro-economic policy; and this preoccupation is likely to
influence union bargaining behaviour. But this merely
establishes that at the national level unions will be involved
in politics over the labour costs/unemployment dilemma.
This does not explain either (a) why they move from that
preoccupation to a general political interest; or (b) why
they usually express that interest by building links with
particular political parties.

Although the former question is logically prior, I shall
deal first here with the question of party identity since that
is more quickly dispatched. Would not unions do better to
enter politics by making demands on whatever is the government of the day, rather than by tying themselves to one
party – somewhat in the manner of Third World countries
playing off Soviet and US interests against each other
while allying with neither? There is some truth in this.
Unions have to remain willing to do business with Conservative governments; and they have to tell Labour governments that they cannot be regarded as simply the
industrial arm of the party. But there is another, larger
question at stake: that of the social bases which can support
the heterogeneity of parties necessary to a competitive
political system; support in the sense of the provision of
blocs of loyalty, of cadres of activists and policy-proposers,
of supportive propaganda and finance. Whatever may be
the attitude of manual and routine non-manual workers to
the unions and to their links with the Labour Party, the fact
remains that no other organizations have appeared in
British society which emerged from the lives of these
people and which try actively to prosecute an interpretation
of their interests where these conflict with others in the
society. To advocate the end of all links between the
Labour Party and the unions is nothing less than to advocate the end of political pluralism in Britain, for there is no
other social cleavage within the society to support a major
degree of party competition than that which is represented

by the conflict between organized labour and capital. (If the new alliance between the Liberal Party and the Social Democratic Party is to become a significant force in politics, it will have to find sources of support and finance, and it will be interesting to see how it does so, to what extent they concern ordinary working people, and what effect the particular pattern found has on the alliance's evolving policies.)

Further, there is little evidence that the conflict between labour and capital is merely an historical legacy, for the past decade has seen a revival of several of the issues at the heart of that conflict, as in the face of the country's economic decline and the international recession such issues as full employment, the welfare state and the nature of managerial prerogatives are again at the top of the political agenda.

It is possible for there to be other major cleavages in societies – such as race, language, religion and national identity – and in many cases these are bases for party formation, though they usually involve some relationship to the labour/capital divide and often also embrace trade-union splits as well.[5] But in Britain, with the marginal exception of Celtic nationalism, no such cleavages exist. The situation is also slightly different in such countries as West Germany and the Scandinavian nations, where political parties receive state subsidies to help them sustain themselves in the absence of rich supporters; but Conservatives have prevented the introduction of such a system here.

The pattern of political involvement

Turning now to the question (a), why do unions acquire a general political involvement, it should not be expected that unions will simply agree to help maintain employment levels by limiting their demands. They will also seek other ways to have employment protected from all kinds of economic adversity; to use their political influence to reduce the severity of the labour-market constraint. A major historical moment in the development of trade-union politics was the 1930s, when economists were developing theories of how the state might intervene, through demand-management and public expenditure policies, to ensure full employment. In Britain these policies were associated with John Maynard Keynes (1936); in Scandinavia with economists close to the Social Democratic and Labour parties. In both instances it was the trade-union movements which took up these policies and pressed them on governments. In the Scandinavian cases, where labour-movement political parties were in office, they had rapid success; in Britain the adoption of Keynesian policies had to wait for their coincidental adoption as part of the mobilization of the war economy. They were then maintained by the post-war Labour and Conservative governments until the late 1970s. Most union movements in the Western world have advocated policies of this kind; that is, policies of government manipulation of tax rates and public spending as well as other forms of state intervention to maintain full employment.

Government action can vitally affect the climate within which unions carry out their primary task; that is enough to explain union involvement in economic policy. Further, if governments are interested in securing union co-operation over wage questions, they will try to press unions into a bargaining relationship with themselves, so that something can be traded for the restraint. If such an arrangement becomes deeply entrenched, as it has, for example, in Austria, or was for a long period in the Scandinavian countries, one may almost lose sight of the bargained nature of it. Unions and government become accustomed to a relationship in which, within a context of close co-operation over policy, they gain many little victories and make many little concessions over an extensive time period.

This has never really happened in Britain, except perhaps for the early years of the post-war Labour government. We have, however, had examples of more short-term, explicit exchanges. The most prominent instance was the Social Contract between Labour and the unions in the late 1970s (see Crouch, 1977; and Panitch, 1976). That government was prepared to grant several union policy demands, especially in three Acts of Parliament which considerably strengthened the rights of both unions and individual workers (the Trade Union and Labour Relations Act 1974, the Employment Protection Act 1975 and an amendment to the former in 1976). This action acquired added significance in that the Conservative opposition at that time was very hostile to trade unions. The unions therefore had strong motives for keeping Labour in office, and between 1975 and 1978 were prepared to restrain wage demands in order to help its counter-inflationary policy. This restraint went so far as to put pressure on either unofficial groupings or, through the TUC, even on official unions which tried to defy the policy. This was exceptional action for British unions, but the times were exceptional; inflation had been rising steadily since the world energy crisis of late 1973 and reached 25 per cent, the highest level in the industrial West. There were deep fears, which union leaders and ordinary workers shared, of a major collapse of the British economy. The co-operation which such a situation engendered did not last indefinitely; by early 1979 shop-floor action in several public services broke the wage-restraint policy. But it is not our present task to retrace that story. The point is to identify the union strategy of co-operation with a government, offering wage restraint and perhaps other concessions in exchange for legislation and the maintenance in office of a government favourable to union interests. This is not the Perlman model of 'pure and simple unionism', limited to free collective bargaining with employers. At the same time it cannot be fitted into the stereotype of union leaders 'selling out' their members by becoming incorporated in an Establishment world; the policy exchange was too substantial, and the economic position too serious, for such an explanation to suffice.

Neo-corporatism

Writers seeking a term to describe such a pattern have
spoken of corporatism. This word has had a strange history
(Schmitter, 1979). It was originated by Roman Catholic
social thinkers in the nineteenth century, trying to find a
compromise between the conflict and individualism of
capitalism on the one hand and the revolutionary challenge
of socialism on the other. The model they developed was
of a society in which – in contrast with capitalism – func-
tional interests were essentially *organized*, but – in contrast
with socialism – these organizations did not engage in a
class struggle to the death, but co-operated in running the
economy. The scope for co-operation would be provided
by a social consensus, preferably based on the unity of the
Catholic faith. In practice, as might be expected, such a
faith provided a slender basis on which to reconcile the
conflicts of capital and labour. In the twentieth century
corporatism reappeared in very different clothes as the
social policy of fascism. First in Mussolini's Italy, then in
Spain and Portugal and, to a much lesser extent, in Nazi
Germany, a corporatist doctrine and practice were developed which found something far more substantial than
religious faith to unite capital and labour; the execution,
imprisonment or persecution of labour leaders and other
opponents, combined with the ideological domination of a
totalitarian state. The 'representative' organs of fascist
corporatism were really little more than façades for control
by the one-party state.

The fascist period discredited the notion of corporatism
in Europe, though it continued to be important to industrial
relations in Latin America, especially during the Peronist
period in Argentina. In political discussion the word is
rarely used other than as a term of abuse. However, during
the past decade it has crept back into academic discussion
to describe a pattern of relations in societies remote from
both Catholic social thought and fascism: the social democ-

racies[6] of northern Europe (Berger, 1981; Crouch, forth-coming; Schmitter and Lehmbruch, 1979)! This is not so bizarre as it seems if we recall the crucial component of the Catholic doctrine: the organization of interests (primarily of capital and labour) on a basis of long-term class co-operation rather than a struggle to the finish. Social democracy (or democratic socialism) has developed as a political force which does not envisage, except perhaps in the indefinitely postponed long term, the abolition of capitalism, but the domestication of it within a context of government economic planning, the welfare state and powerful trade unions. As such, social democracy believes in organized class interests of capital and labour which will co-operate in a long-term national interest. Their co-operation is ensured, not by a religious faith as in the Catholic doctrine, but by a detailed web of compromises in which, for example, labour gains a welfare state and progressive taxation while capital gains the assistance of labour's organizations in subordinating labour to industrial authority. The major distinctions between this 'social democratic' corporatism and both the classical and fascist forms is often acknowledged through the term 'neo-corporatism'.

I am not concerned here to argue whether such an arrangement is good or desirable, or whether such a pattern of co-operation between antagonistic interests can last indefinitely. I am simply trying to show how, in the context of social democracy, a pattern of industrial relations seems to develop which does have some strange similarities with nineteenth-century Catholic ideas of corporatism; a fascinating irony given the old antagonism between socialism and Catholicism.

Neo-corporatist relations, like collective bargaining, concern organized actors, primarily of workers and employers. But unlike collective bargaining, the organizations are trying to find a positive sum game; that is, they are looking for points of co-operation where they might both gain something; they are not simply bargaining over the distribution of a fixed sum of potential gains. If this happens at national level it is virtually certain to involve the state. First, the government cannot be indifferent to large organized groups covering the whole country and proceeding to make national-level decisions about the economy. Second, it is probably a condition of union co-operation in such an arrangement that a democratic government will be willing to pursue policies, such as full employment, which are favourable to workers' interests (Stephens, 1979). This does not mean that government will be constantly intervening in relations between the employers and the unions; if they seem willing to take its advice and pursue policies which it favours, it may well be content to stay on the sidelines, maintaining a close watching brief. The point is that, whether the government is active or not, unions engaged in this kind of national-level action over economic policy have moved out of the field of ordinary collective bargaining and have entered politics. What are the stakes in this kind of action for organized labour? How does it affect our analysis in the preceding chapter of the different positions of different levels within the labour movement?

The level of labour actor most important to national corporatism, the *confederation* of unions, was not considered in chapter 5. In the most enduring instances of this kind of corporatism (in Scandinavia, the Netherlands and Austria), much ordinary wage bargaining is conducted by these confederations rather than by individual unions; it is notable that these are all small countries. This means that a substantive goal of direct, immediate interest to individual workers is a prominent item on the agenda of the national-level bodies. In a country like Britain, where no bargaining takes place at the level of the TUC, the confederal level is immediately of diminished interest to individual workers. But in any event, much of the business of national forums concerns long-term goals, such as the maintenance of full employment, which are indirect and uncertain in their implications for individuals and for the shop-floor organization. Further, governments prefer to

have only a very small number of actors, the confederations
or peak associations, active at the national level. They do
this for several reasons. Partly, it is simply a matter of
efficiency, of reducing the number of communications that
a government department has to make. But, more important, it is a means of delegating regulation, which is crucial
to corporatism. If a matter on which unions have conflicting views can be agreed at the level of the confederation,
then presumably that organization will ensure compliance
among its members with the agreed policy; as we have
noted, the British Social Contract worked briefly in exactly
that way. But if confederations are going to play that role,
their member associations need to have a strong motive for
remaining affiliated to them; what if dissident member
unions simply 'exit'? Assuming that it is not possible for
governments to make confederal affiliation compulsory,
they will nevertheless try to ensure that it is attractive to
individual unions and that there are few rewards for those
who remain unaffiliated. They can do this by offering
participation goals; by offering membership of a range of
decision-making or consultative forums to the confederation, and by maintaining those forums as the only channel
by which they communicate with organized labour. If an
individual union wants to pursue an issue covered by such
a forum, it can do so only by being a member of the
confederation. The Social Contract phase in Britain saw a
multiplication of such activity. Government consulted
closely with the TUC over a wide range of policies, and
also established such bodies as the Advisory, Conciliation
and Arbitration Service, which had the power to decide
certain inter-union recognition disputes, and on the governing body of which the TUC was represented. Not
surprisingly, these years saw a number of trade unions
which had previously stood aloof from the TUC become
affiliated to it.

Overall, therefore, the effect of unions becoming involved in national economic policy questions is to shift
their proceedings away from both the issues and the levels

in which individual workers and, perhaps even more so, shop-floor organizations are interested. The participation available is limited to the national level, and may even be at the explicit or implicit expense of local participation (as, for example, in the institution of national tripartite incomes policies). They are also more likely to satisfy participation goals than money goals; they are probably offering the participation as an alternative to money gains, which they are trying to reduce; and if they favour any money gains they will be those at the controllable centralized national level. One solution which unions can and do adopt to tackle this problem is to use the political exchange with government to win participation rights for the shop-floor level (see chapter 5, note 5).

There are several reasons for assuming that unions will accept participation in relations with government – and the commitment to restraint which this at least in principle implies. As organizations, they gain directly from measures which enhance their potential power to affect decisions (Pizzorno, 1978), though their willingness to do this in any particular case will depend on certain factors. We have already seen how both willingness to participate and the effectiveness of any participation will depend on the degree of centralization of the union movement. We should also expect the decision-making effectiveness of the forum concerned to be important; unions are likely to concede more to gain participation the more important the forum concerned. Further, we might expect past experience and the ideological dispositions of union leaders to matter here; the decisions concerned are long-term, uncertain ones in which precise knowledge is often unavailable. In such circumstances people fall back on experience and/or unquestioned beliefs in order to decide the likely relationships between available means and ends. Finally, links between parties and unions may be relevant; where the government concerned is formed from a party or parties with whom the union leaders have strong links, we may expect their actions to be governed partly by party considerations.

So far these points have all concerned the union as organization. The members do not share the union's direct interest in participation *per se*; they are not involved in detailed links between governments, unions, employers and political parties. To the extent that they have the power to do so, members are likely to resist the agreements for wage restraint which their leaders make with governments. This does not mean that they do not believe inflation to be a problem in which union action is in some way implicated. But, as we have noted, given their fragmented position, they are unable to take action in that collective interest. Hence the frequently encountered paradox that opinion polls report a widespread aversion to strikes and high wage claims, even to trade unions themselves, among workers who strike in pursuit of their own claims.[7] The problem of the logic of collective action hits with double force at this level of national economic developments: the arena of action is one in which the unions, themselves collectivities, are participating as actors in another collectivity.

These problems apply, not just to a situation in which unions exchange restraint for the power goal of participation, but also to the few cases where the goals are economic ones. The economic ends which can be secured by governments are either long-term (e.g., the improvements in real incomes which might follow from concerted action in restraining inflation) or collective (e.g., social welfare policies, increasingly known as the 'social wage'). In the case of the former, members are in no position to assess their feasibility, while the latter are subject to the usual problems of collective goods. In both cases, therefore, it has to be left to the union to act as guarantor of the members' long-term and collective interests to act on their behalf. It does so, not so much because it directly seeks these goals, because, as we have seen, the union has no money goals unless its officials seek them for value reasons, but because it 'converts' the money goals into the participation goal of its own capacity to help secure them. Thus, while such things as a long-term rise in real incomes and increased social benefits might seem to be a working-class interest, they are interests which unions are unable to follow directly, while the manner in which the national union organization seeks them – as a by-product of its own participation goal – is likely to lead to the familiar division between union leaders and members.

As already suggested, national union involvement in politics is likely to cause even more trouble for relations between national unions and shop-floor organizations. National unions and individual members at least share an interest in nationally negotiated pay rises which by-pass the shop-floor organization. Deals with governments are likely to reinforce the national component of wage increases, because it is at that level that there can be more effective national-political control. Since a central aim of tripartite control is wage restraint, the burden of restraint will be disproportionately borne by those negotiating shop-floor supplements. Governments, employers' peak organizations and union leaderships share an interest in ensuring this, and workers must be assumed to be relatively indifferent to the source of their wage rises, so the main net loser from wage-restraint agreements is the shop-floor organization. This does not necessarily mean that this organization is some kind of parasitical body with which the workers can easily dispense; it may well be that in the long run workers will suffer from a lack of protection at plant level if the shop-floor organization declines and is not there to help them.

An outstanding example of this process occurred during the great French strikes of May 1968. This strike movement, organized at the shop floor, embarrassed the government and employers for obvious reasons; but it was also a problem for the largely communist leadership of the national unions, who were left out of it all. The Gaullist government and the communist confederation, the Confédération Générale du Travail, who usually had little to do with each other, suddenly found they had a shared goal in eclipsing the shop-floor movement. They realized that goal by agreeing to a nationwide pay increase. For the government this quelled the disruption; for the CGT it restored to itself the capacity to make gains for the workers.

In general, therefore, we should expect shop-floor organizations to oppose corporatism. There are plenty of historical examples of this. As Panitch (1981: 35) has pointed out:

> ... what characterizes the development of corporatist structures, no less than their persistence, in certain bourgeois democracies, is their instability. The corporatist-structured incomes policies of Britain and Sweden in the late 1940s were defeated by the labour movement at the turn of the decade, and although resuscitated quickly in Sweden, in Britain they were not really revived until the Conservative government established the tripartite National Economic Development Council in 1961 to secure trade-union participation in an incomes policy. (In Holland, the initial post-war policies of corporatist economic planning had lasted longer, but rank-and-file pressure led to a renegotiation of the basis of incomes policy in 1959 and the rejection of centralized wage controls by 1963.) But it was the outbreak of rank-and-file militancy throughout Europe in the late 1960s that really demonstrated the fragility of corporatist political structures. This militancy, being a general phenomenon after the recession of 1966-7, cannot, of course, be attributed only to the resentment against corporatist wage-restraint policies. But where they existed, resentment against them certainly fuelled militancy and became a focal point for mobilization.

It was well-organized craftsmen who resented the erosion of their differentials over less skilled workers who broke union support for wage restraint in Britain in 1950. In the late 1960s it was not just the inability of incomes policy to control shop-floor bargaining, but also the fact that by then several major union leaders had themselves emerged from the shop-floor movement and remained dependent on it for support, that broke incomes policy. The same phenomenon reappeared in 1978, culminating in the winter of discontent at the start of 1979.

Often, shop-floor leaders will be able to carry their members with them, though if the national-level activity is producing enough gains the workers may be content to accept it. Whether or not the national unions are successful in prolonging relations with government and employers at national level will depend partly on what they are able to deliver through such forums, but partly on the structure of the union movement. If it is one in which power is centralized, it will be easier to sustain national action. If, as in Britain, the power of the movement is skewed towards the base, these understandings will constantly be upset. It must be noted that a powerful shop-floor movement has the power to frustrate national-level activity even though it does not itself act on the national stage. If national understandings are constantly broken on the union side by autonomous action at the plant level, the national unions are unable to deliver industrial peace, which is what they have to offer government, and therefore government becomes less interested in making deals with them. One of the several reasons why the present Conservative government in Britain is ignoring the TUC and relying on high unemployment to keep wages restrained is that on several occasions union behaviour has implied that it is not worthwhile reaching deals with them since their agreements will be upset by autonomous shop-floor action.

The paradox of unions' political goals

The analysis here has concentrated on unions' and workers' problems in reconciling the means available to them with their aims of preserving long-term rises in real incomes alongside high employment levels. A similar analysis applies, however, if we see union political demands in a more assertive light and concentrate more on what they are trying to gain through political action, rather than simply on what they are trying to exchange in a deal over wage restraint. Unions do indeed have many such goals, and they feature strongly in their rhetoric: improvements in unions' own and workers' legal rights against employers; general economic policies favourable to labour; social and educational policies that will be in the interests of workers and their families. Where improvements in unions' and workers' employment rights are concerned, there are few problems, and unions do indeed pursue these strongly. But the wider goals suffer from a disadvantage we have already noted: while they are all in the interests of the members, they are such only indirectly or in the long term. In particular, no gains from such demands are experienced in a manner which enables workers to make a direct connection between union action and outcome.[8] The union's own interests are also indirect; it gains by the fact of participating in the pursuit of the demands (though this has to be offset against the surrender of power in bargaining and probably consequent tension with the membership), but it is likely to gain little in terms of members' gratitude for any substantive outcome. In particular, it is doubtful if the union could wield any industrial strength in the pursuit of these goals. Since some of the unions' stated economic goals, such as giving unions and government the central role in making investment decisions, involve a challenge to the capitalist economy, this will be a severe handicap.

We therefore have a vivid paradox: a series of intrinsically important activities are undertaken by unions quite logically and sensibly, within important national forums in dialogue with the state, but at the same time not really seriously. Unions will not stand or fall in the eyes of their membership by their performance in these areas, and while demands will be raised and argued about, they are unlikely to be pressed under the threat of industrial action in the way that wage demands are.

All this helps explain the process which was witnessed in several countries in the 1970s. Organized workers established a strength against employers and governments of a kind not witnessed before for many years. They were able to make their bargaining demands effective and, at various moments in France, Italy and the United Kingdom, threatened the stability of the politico-economic system. But this power led to few major social changes. Certainly, and as we would expect, most union movements used their new power to gain extensions in unions' own rights and those of shop-floor organizations and of their members against employers, and these have been significant. But demands for wider changes in economic and social policy were far less successful. For example, in the early 1970s the Italian unions tried to mobilize national strike action for improvements in housing policy and health services; but there was little response to the call, and by 1974 they had fallen back on a defensive policy of avoiding unemployment (Regalia et al., 1978: 132–6, 153–4).

It is true that international economic developments became markedly unfavourable from 1973 onwards, but that does not by itself satisfactorily explain labour's failure to take advantage of the apparent power which it had developed since the late 1960s, or its inability, seen most vividly in Britain, to deploy its power in anything more constructive than a self-defeating pursuit of wage rises which stimulated inflation and eventually raised unemployment. It is here that paying attention to the different positions of union leaderships, shop-floor organizations and membership is important. Of course, many observers would accept that statement, but would see the difference as either one of a leadership betraying its members, or alternatively as a foolish membership and shop-floor organization not following their leaders' enlightened strategy. The analysis adopted here has tried to provide a more objective and realistic approach. For the labour movement to have taken full advantage of the new militancy of its members and strength of its organizations which developed in the late 1960s and early 1970s it would have had to be capable of acting at least at the level of the national political economy; and probably at the virtually inaccessible international level. But the great strength of the labour movement in that period lay precisely in its decentralized and mass-participative nature. The disparity in the logic of action at these levels has been the contemporary tragedy of the labour movement.

At the political as much as at the industrial level much can be learned of why various labour actors behave the way they do by looking at the logic of their situation, inspecting the means available to them to pursue their goals and the social context which provides them with a more or less limited set of opportunities and constraints.

This can be demonstrated by comparing the assessment I have made here of the likely gains and losses for organized labour from neo-corporatist arrangements with the different one which flows from a Marxist account of labour's situation and potential power. In a recent paper on corporatism in industrial relations, Panitch (1981) rejects the possibility of unions using these arrangements to make advances for working-class interests by pointing out how, in Britain, Sweden and Germany, unions during the 1970s were forced into increasingly defensive positions within corporatist contexts:

Each of these corporatist wage policies were negotiated in years of national economic crisis of proportions unknown in the postwar period. And corporatist political structures became the vehicle for engineering, legitimating ('in the national interest') and administering the increase in exploitation which was necessary to sustain capital in the crisis. The sacrifice undertaken by the working class in the context of the crisis would have been one thing had the respective governments implemented those reflationary policies and structural reforms which the union movements had promulgated earlier in the 1970s. That they were undertaken rather in the context of policies which were designed to restore the profitability of private capital and which depended on *this* to reduce unemployment, is an indication that only class collaboration, not class struggle, can be practised in the corporatist 'heart' of the state apparatus. In so far as class struggle was practised, it was not within, but outside of an [*sic*] implicitly or explicitly against, corporatist structures, as seen most clearly in the strikes of 1978–9 in West Germany and Britain, and of 1980 in Sweden. [p. 38]

Panitch is here mainly arguing against those Marxists who have seen scope in neo-corporatism for major advances in working-class power and social transformation. In so doing he uses an account of the role of unions not dissimilar to that developed here:

> ... unions by their very nature cannot undertake such a transformation on their own, being constituted, as they are, on the basis of mobilizing workers for short-term gains *within* capitalism. This ... does account for the relative low ordering in their operative priorities usually given to public ownership and controls over capital.... [*ibid*: 43]

My disagreement really starts when *alternatives* are discussed. First, there is the alternative of what would have happened had unions not co-operated with corporatist plans in the mid-1970s. Panitch's account of the compromises made by union leaders at that time fails to mention the single viable political alternative being presented, at least in the British case: a total reliance by government on restriction of the money supply in order, at whatever economic cost, to squeeze inflation out of the system by increasing unemployment until the capacity of organized labour to make effective demands was weakened. To assert this is not idle speculation; it is what has happened following the collapse of the neo-corporatist experiment in Britain in 1979. Further, while stressing, accurately, that wages were restricted to save the level of profits, he has nothing to say on how investment might be increased or inflation reduced without wage restraint.

Panitch goes on to point out, again accurately, that following the strikes of winter 1979, the TUC and the Labour government tried to salvage a corporatist arrangement in a document with the highly corporatist heading: 'The Economy, the Government and Trade Union Responsibilities', which set out ways in which unions would

try to restrain strike pickets, abide by disputes-procedures,
maintain emergency services during strikes and allow flexibility in the operation of the closed shop. In this way, he
says:

> the TUC General Council *publicly* legitimated, and associated
> the working class with legitimating, the general interest of the
> bourgeoisie and the government regarding the strikes then
> taking place. [*ibid*: 42]

What he fails to point out is that the conduct of pickets
during those strikes caused more resentment of trade
unions among working people than any event in living
memory, immediately and directly strengthening working-
class support for a Conservative opposition which was
promising legislation on picketing and the closed shop.
That was the detailed context of the decisions being
faced by union leaders in the 1975–9 period, and it is not
helpful to try to account for the actions which they took by
simply setting out the more remote rival logics of sustain-
ing capitalism or undertaking revolutionary advance.'

This brings us to the second sense in which the choices
facing unions should be considered; the resources available
to the unions to act. 'To warn against the dangers of further
trade-union integration into the capitalist state is not to
return to a syndicalist position,' asserts Panitch (p. 43); the
union movement has to be kept out of corporatist entangle-
ments so that a revolutionary working-class party might be
developed. It is one thing as an intellectual position to
reject syndicalism as well as corporatism in favour of a
revolutionary working class; but if you are a trade-union
official in contemporary Britain, you do not have even the
embryo of a revolutionary working class anywhere re-
motely near you. You do have a good deal of syndicalism,
in the shape of shop-floor activity entirely uninterested in
politics, and you do have the prospect of mass unemployment as a possible political response to union power. That
is the context within which union action takes place. To
construct an entire theory of trade unionism around a non-

existent phenomenon – the revolutionary working class – is to produce something of limited usefulness in understanding the real day-to-day choices of trade unions and their members. But that is what Marxist sociology has chosen to do.

To take this line of argument does not mean that one must maintain that union action is only relevant to the minutiae of industrial decision-making, but simply to take issue with the particular framework within which Marxism chooses to interpret union action. True, a large amount of union behaviour *is* concerned with minutiae, as reflected in the earlier chapters of this book: the decisions confronting workers whether or not to join a union, how long to keep up a strike, whether to go for a wage demand or seek improvements in job control. But occasionally the decisions made by unions, whether at a national level or emerging from a cumulative mass of everyday actions, reverberate more widely and have major ramifications for national politics. The past few years have been such a time in industrial relations particularly in Britain but also elsewhere, and the dust has yet to settle.

Notes

1. Approaches to the Study of Trade Unions

1. The clearest and most compendious guide to industrial relations in Britain is Clegg (1979); the more theoretical counterpart of which is Flanders (1970). Hyman (1975) is a Marxist 'alternative' to an earlier edition of Clegg; Hyman (1972) and Allen (1971) are further Marxist introductions. Eldridge (1968 and 1971), Jackson (1977) and, from a German perspective, Beyme (1977) are more explicitly sociological contributions. Hughes (1968) and Poole (1981) deal specifically with trade unions, the latter providing a valuable survey of different sociological approaches. Useful collections of basic readings are McCarthy (1972), Nichols (1980) and Clarke and Clements (1977), the latter two being largely Marxist.

2. In 1971 the Conservative government wanted to know how strong was support among postmen for the national strike which had been launched by the Union of Post-Office Workers. Knowledge of the workers' capacity to withstand a prolonged strike was crucial to the government's strategy in the dispute. It therefore approached several academic industrial-relations specialists to ask them to do a piece of research on support for the strike. Nearly all those approached refused the project.

3. The significance of Vauxhall Motors at Luton was that this factory had been the subject of a major piece of sociological research, initially published in Goldthorpe (1966), and later in Goldthorpe, Lockwood *et al.* (1968a and b; 1969), a central theme of which had been the unlikelihood of sustained revolutionary consciousness, as opposed to instrumental militancy, among such workers, who were seen as essentially accepting their subordination to management. When workers at the same plant rioted, sang the Red Flag and called for directors to be 'strung up', Blackburn wrote:

> Rarely can a sociological study such as this have been so cruelly put to the test. Scarcely one month after the publication of Goldthorpe's

findings, on 17 and 18 October 1966, the Luton car workers broke into open rebellion. The workers in whom Goldthorpe had been able to detect 'little tendency to interpret employer-worker relations in fundamentally "oppositional terms"' were responsible for an outbreak.... [1967: 48]

Since then, the case has been cited in innumerable undergraduate essays on the revolutionary potentialities of the British working class; meanwhile, unnoticed, the Luton workers have returned to the pattern of industrial relations which Goldthorpe described and have acquired no subsequent reputation for radicalism. As Mann has asked of the same event: 'Dramatic as this appears, however, did it leave any aftermath? The strike subsided days later when specific grievances were settled' (1973: 47). And, as he also points out (p. 45), the Goldthorpe and Lockwood account allowed for the kind of ambiguity in workers' consciousness that could lead to paradoxical behaviour of this kind.

4. It is not just a question of wages. Many union actions, such as job control and insistence on certain manning levels, workspeeds, etc., involve increases in unit labour costs equivalent to wage rises in their effect on production costs.

5. For extensive discussions of problems of exchange and rational choice in social theory that go beyond what is possible here, see the excellent accounts in Blau (1964), Barry (1970) and Heath (1976). For an approach which combines aspects of rational choice with a more orthodox Weberian sociology, see Eldridge, 1971: 40–63.

6. The term 'social actor' is a useful shorthand phrase, provided it is understood. Normally the unit of action in a social exchange is a collectivity: a trade union did this; a group of workers did that; a government did something else. In each of these and many similar cases, a large number of different individual persons were involved, and their individual contributions to the action in question may well have differed slightly from each other; but for the purposes of analysis it makes sense to treat them as one unit. 'Social actor' is therefore a *collective* noun; it does not refer to an *individual* human being. This is perhaps also the best place to explain that it is purely grammatical convention that renders the appropriate pronoun for social actor as 'he'. Not only are social actors in reality plural persons; many of them are in fact social actresses.

2. The Drive to Combine

1. Some evidence of the continuing role of selective incentives in membership recruitment, and also of an important modern change in their nature, could be found in a recent advertisement by the National Union of Dyers, Bleachers and Textile Workers. The union claimed

that it had achieved nearly £1,000,000 in benefits for *individual*
members during the course of a year; in accident benefit,
unemployment benefit, strike pay, death and loss of limb benefit *and*
'compensation obtained by the union's solicitors in respect of
industrial accidents'. What is notable is that over half the total sum
(£508,393) was accounted for by this last category. As state action and
legal rights have both taken over certain kinds of social assistance
formerly provided by unions and extended the range of available
benefits, unions have found a new role in helping their members claim
benefits due to them. The importance of this as a selective benefit
should not be overlooked. When we find evidence of a union
demanding legislation to improve workers' rights in some respect, we
might initially regard this as a pure example of the pursuit of a public
good; but if the union will subsequently have a prominent role in
helping individual members claim the new right, it may in fact serve
as a selective incentive to membership.

2. The distinction between closed and open unions (Turner, 1962) is
relevant here. A closed union recruits from a highly selected category
of workers – usually craftsmen or professionals – and is devoted to
protecting their privileges, membership of the union usually being
essential to claim the privilege. Such unions are less likely to
experience the Olsonian problem than are open unions, which recruit
all-comers from a large mass, membership of the union conferring no
automatic advantages. Within wider sociological theory, the
phenomenon of unions which use a closed membership to advance
their members' position is a case of the 'closure' practised by social
classes described by Parkin (1974). He points out that classes, or parts
of classes, may be 'open' (in the sense that access to them by people
from diverse backgrounds is easy and unimpeded) or 'closed'
(meaning that barriers have either been deliberately erected or
emerged, which are then exploited by existing class members to
restrict entry, partly to exploit scarcity value and partly to ensure that
new entrants come from the same social groups, or even the same
families, as existing members). High prestige often flows from
successful pursuit of this strategy, as the class becomes recognized as
'exclusive' and distinctive. It is a device usually associated with highly
privileged elites, but within the ranks of manual labour the same
process can be seen working through this form of closed unionism.
The aim is usually market advantage through scarcity and also
prestige, rather than dynastic succession, though the last is not
unknown when unions have a particularly powerful voice in deciding
labour recruitment. Examples have been the London docks (now
almost entirely closed down) and the printing industry in Fleet Street;
in both cases jobs have gone to successive generations from the same
families.

3. According to the most recent research (Gennard *et al.*, 1980), the

proportion of workers in closed shops has risen from the 17 per cent found by McCarthy (1964) in the early 1960s to around 23 per cent in 1978. Since the proportion of the workforce in union membership has increased during that period, the rise in the closed shop is not striking. However, one important fact is that the earlier study found the closed shop concentrated in certain industries – mining, metal manufacture, engineering, ship-building and printing – which have been declining since the 1960s. So if the overall proportion of workers in closed shops has been rising, there must have been considerable increases in some sectors. There remains considerable variation in incidence: from 87 per cent in coal mining, 80 per cent in gas, water and electricity, and 66 per cent in paper, printing and publishing, to 5 per cent in insurance, banking and business finance, 3 per cent in professional and scientific services, and 1 per cent in agriculture, forestry and fishing. The closed shop remains far more common in manual (one third) than in non-manual (one tenth) employment. The original form of closed shop, the pre-entry shop, now accounts for only 20 per cent of closed-shop membership.

4. In its evidence to the Donovan Commission in 1965, the TUC claimed:

> The fact that trade unions in Britain have succeeded through their own efforts in strengthening their organization and in obtaining recognition, not relying on the assistance of the Government through legislation, is one of the most important factors sustaining their strength and independence. Trade unions have not been given privileges; they have fought for what they have achieved. [Royal Commission, 1968b: para 308]

5. The main reason for the change seems to have been the unions' growing confidence that they could exercise political power without much fear of a disadvantageous *quid pro quo*, perhaps coupled with a realization that, since government involvement in industrial relations seemed to have become a permanent feature anyway, they may as well seek what gains they could within such a framework. In 1969 the unions had not only forced the withdrawal of the Labour government's attempt at imposing minor legislative controls on them, but had also seen that government's incomes policy in retreat (Crouch, 1979: ch. 3). By 1972 it was becoming clear that they could mount effective resistance to the Conservative government's far tougher Industrial Relations Act 1971 (Moran, 1977), and that both that government and the Labour opposition were desperate to work in agreement with the TUC (Crouch, 1979: 83–90). It was at this time that the unions were formulating their new legislative demands on union rights from a future Labour government. However, it should be noted that a residual fear of legal entanglement over recognition survived. At TUC insistence, the Labour government's legislation of

1974–6 fell short of imposing a clear duty on employers to recognize unions; a loop-hole which was later used to devastating effect by employers resisting the unionization of their employees, in particular the notorious Grunwick case discussed earlier in this chapter (Rogaly, 1978: esp. ch. 11).

6. The Trade Union and Labour Relations Act 1974; the Employment Protection Act 1975; and the Trade Union and Labour Relations (Amendment) Act 1976.

3. The Means of Collective Action

1. A sizeable number of people on low incomes do in fact depend on investment earnings; for example, many elderly widows and unmarried daughters of businessmen. However, these people are rarely in a position to affect the decisions made by the companies from which they gain their small incomes.

2. In modern conditions we rarely observe strikes which can reduce workers to destitution and near-starvation, but in the nineteenth century and earlier years of the present one it was no rare occurrence. For two fictional but highly realistic accounts, see John Galsworthy's play *Strife* and Emile Zola's novel *Germinal*. Both bring out the appalling difficulties faced by workers trying to make rational decisions about their interests in conditions of desperation and great lack of knowledge of the situation of the employer.

3. Questions are often raised about the rationality of union behaviour on the many occasions when the wage increase gained at the end of a strike is far smaller than the earnings lost by the workers in the course of it. Can such a strike make sense? One answer may be that the workers miscalculated both the length of the strike and the size of the eventual wage gain, though their original expectations on these scores may have been quite reasonable gambles. Some observers (e.g., Boulding, 1963: 217) have suggested that a strike is not so much a calculative event as an explosion of feelings and resentments; that is, a fundamentally non-rational act. However, we do not necessarily need to make that assumption. As the nineteenth-century economist Alfred Marshall argued, there is a political or organizational rationality involved in industrial conflict as well as a straight economic rationality, though in the long run the two may be the same:

> ... there is no advantage in comparing the expense of any particular strike with the total direct gain to wages ... because a strike is a mere incident in a campaign, and the policy of keeping up an army and entering a campaign has to be judged as a whole. The gain of

any particular battle is not to be measured by the booty got in it.
[1899: 379]
This draws attention to the difference between the individualized
gains in wages which may come from a strike and the collective gain to
the union which follows from the demonstration of its power. For
workers to accept the latter goal, the organization has had to resolve
favourably the Olsonian problem. For an extended discussion of the
rationale of striking, see Hyman (1972: ch. 5), from which the
references to Boulding and Marshall have been drawn.
4. When matters do come to a head in such a system, conflict may be
very wide indeed. This was shown in Sweden in 1980 when, after
years of exceptionally low industrial conflict, a general strike virtually
brought the economy to a halt for several days. For more information
on Swedish unions see Elvander (1979), Ingham (1974), Jackson and
Sisson (1976); on German unions see Bergmann *et al.* (1975), Müller-
Jentsch and Sperling (1978), Streeck (1980).
5. This larger question of class relations is somewhat beyond the
scope of the present volume, but the assumption that working-class
affluence and the emergence of managerial capitalism led to any
fundamental change in class relations has been strongly contested by
other sociologists. See, on the former point, Goldthorpe, Lockwood *et
al.* (1969); on the latter, Blackburn (1965); and on both, Westergaard
and Resler (1975).
6. In comparison with earlier capitalist society, far more income is
now derived from state benefits, pensions, etc. Some authors have
argued that this may shift the locus of conflict from industry to
politics, and therefore away from the scope of industrial relations
(Hibbs, 1978). This is an interesting and complex argument. However,
it remains the case that for the great majority of people income from
employment constitutes a far greater share of total lifetime income than
do state benefits. Further, state benefits are financed from taxation, and
there is at least some evidence that increases in taxation lead to workers'
making increased wage claims, thereby potentially increasing
industrial conflict (Wilkinson and Turner, 1972). The occupational
system remains the major source of workers' income.

4. Union Goals

1. Capitalism depends for its dominance, not on rule by a clearly
defined class of persons, but on the sovereignty of a particular *process*:
the allocation of goods and services by largely free market forces, the
means for competition within the market being primarily in private
hands. This has historically given it a capacity for absorbing rising
social forces and for moulding itself to changing power balances
within society not possessed by forms of domination dependent on the

formal power position of distinct social groups (e.g., feudalism). (For similar arguments, see Giddens, 1973: ch. 10.)

2. A far larger number, of course, regularly attempts the football pools. But the precise attraction of the pools is that the time, effort and money needed to participate is minimal in comparison with that required for other human activities with similarly ambitious ends in view. It is certainly a lot easier than running a shop, successfully occupying a batting crease or organizing a revolution.

3. While bargaining does not assume even a rough equality of power, it does imply that each side has *some* capacity at least for making life tiresome for the other, so that it is worthwhile trying to come to mutually tolerable terms. Where one side is so weak that this does not arise, bargaining in low-trust contexts is replaced by unilateral imposition supported by surveillance and threats of discipline. In industrial relations the employer's side is virtually the only one with any chance of being in such a dominant position.

4. While recession may cause temporary drops in real wages, the overall tendency in industrial societies is towards increasing standards of living. Even in slowly growing economies, constant minor improvements are made in technology and working methods, including the rising skill level of the workforce which is acquired by experience. These improvements make possible gradual improvements in the rewards from work (for an historical account of the importance of this to rises in the standard of living of British workers, see Phelps Brown with Browne, 1964).

5. While we correctly think mainly of unionization as the source of collective action, even workers not in union membership develop group pressures and informal organization to reduce some of their vulnerability to technical and managerial regulation. A well-known example is the informal pressure exercised against 'rate busters' – workers who work faster and harder than the work-group considers desirable (Roethlisberger *et al.*, 1939).

5. The Union as an Organization

1. A similar arrangement can be found in Britain today within the Civil and Public Services Association, which has rival and well-organized left- and right-wing factions which put up opposing candidates for election to union offices at all levels.

2. In a rather different context, Crozier (1964) has spoken of the dependence of superior levels in a bureaucratic hierarchy on junior levels, the former needing supplies of information, etc. from the latter. While this will not serve as a good analogy for relations between union leaders and members, it does tell us something important about

relations between national union leaders and their regional and local officials.

3. Even within the tightly organized German system there are exceptions. Policemen and railway engine drivers are examples of groups who have a choice between membership of a specialized professional association (or *Beamtenbund*) and that of a generalized union, for public-service workers and railway employees, respectively.

4. Parts of the Industrial Relations Act 1971 assumed the former view, and tried to strengthen the powers of union leaderships to discipline and control their members. The Employment Act 1982, on the other hand, seems to assume that leaders are the main source of militancy, as it places considerable weight on strengthening balloting systems for membership approval of leadership actions.

5. It is quite possible for a national leadership to negotiate participation gains *for* a shop-floor organization, while the reverse is highly unlikely to occur. Important examples in recent years have been the inclusion, following official union pressure, of elected shop-floor representatives in machinery for monitoring health and safety questions at work under the Health and Safety at Work Act 1974; and the negotiation in 1978 by the German metal-working union (IG Metall) of rights of works councils (*Betriebsräte*) in Baden-Württenberg to participate in the management of firms' manpower policies. Whether these cases are clear refutations of the conventional assumption of a difference of interest between levels of union organization, or simply demonstrate the means by which leaderships try to ensure that emergent shop-floor power develops under their control, can be determined only by research.

6. To show how this can become a real problem one may cite the case of Italy, where the recently developed and powerful shop-floor movement has frequently shown signs of entirely ignoring the national unions. Factors explaining this phenomenon include (i) the recency of a strong national union movement in Italy, and (ii) the fact that the formal unions are divided on political and religious lines that make little sense to workers on the shop floor.

6. The Inevitability of Politics

1. This union has recently changed its name to the Union of Communication Workers.

2. A legal case between a trade union and a railway company, in which the judges used Common Law arguments to limit unions' immunity from legal liability for actions taken in the course of an industrial dispute. The precedent set by this decision would have considerably weakened union rights and could be changed only by an Act of Parliament clearly setting out the extent of union immunities. This realization of their dependence on parliamentary action was a major factor in persuading many British union leaders that they needed to be certain of a bloc of sympathetic MPs. They began to give more active support to the infant Labour Party (founded in 1900). In the general election of 1906 thirty Labour MPs were elected. The Liberal Party, which won a landslide majority in that election, at that time regarded the Labour Party as virtually its own offspring, and in 1906 passed the Trade Disputes Act which met labour's demands after Taff Vale (see Pelling, 1976).

3. Britain is also unusual in that the Labour Party's formal system of decision-making is dominated by trade-union block votes. This peculiarity is not under discussion here, but for an analysis of it see Crouch, 1982.

4. The term originated in Sweden (see Robinson, 1974). For a similar analysis applied to West Germany, see Streeck, 1980.

5. A clear if rather extreme example is Belgium, where the linguistic, regional and economic split between Flanders and Wallonia produces divisions between parties superimposed on the more familiar division between Christian Democrats, Socialists and Liberals. In the Netherlands, while a strong Labour Party and associated trade-union movement exist, the division of the population into Catholic, Evangelical, Calvinist and non-religious groupings (some with associated trade-union movements) overlays normal political divisions. This deprives the Labour Party of much of its potential class-bound support, but at the same time imparts to some of the religious parties support for social policies normally monopolized by social democratic parties (for more detailed analyses, see Lijphart, 1976).

The USA is an extreme case of a different kind: the strength of regional and ethnic divisions in mobilizing political loyalties was so strong as completely to override the political alignments familiar to European politics.

6. I here use the term 'social democracy' in the sense normal in discussions of comparative European politics: to describe major labour-movement parties which are not communist. It is doubtful whether the new British Social Democratic Party is a social democratic party in this sense, as it has no links with the union movement and seems to be defining itself as a party hostile to union involvement in politics. The British Labour Party *is* a social democratic party in the generally accepted sense of the term (Paterson and Thomas, 1977).

7. There has been considerable evidence from opinion polls in recent years that even supporters of the Labour Party have become hostile to trade unions and to their role in politics (for example, see Crewe, 1982).

8. A good example is retirement pensions. In the bargaining over the Social Contract in the mid-1970s a crucial role was played by Jack Jones, general secretary of the TGWU. He was one of those union leaders who had emerged from the shop-steward movement, and the support of his union (Britain's largest) was crucial to the government. One of the causes for which Jack Jones had long worked was the improvement of old-age pensions. A major improvement in pensions was instituted by the government in the months before Jones became the Social Contract's main supporter. No doubt other factors also contributed to the pensions policy, but Jones's role is very interesting. However, how many workers, annoyed by wage restraint in the following three years, would have weighed in the balance the possibility that that restraint had helped to secure a higher standard of living for their own aged relatives and, in a number of years' time, themselves? The fact that one cannot *prove* that without Jones's role in the Social Contract the pensions' reform would have been less impressive further demonstrates the difficulty of assessing social gains of this kind.

9. At the time of the 1979 general election 90 per cent of manual workers in Britain supported a legal ban on secondary picketing (Crewe, 1982: 27).

Bibliography

ABERCROMBIE, N., HILL, S. AND TURNER, B. S., 1980, *The Dominant Ideology Thesis* (London: Allen and Unwin)

ALLEN, V. L., 1957, *Trade Union Leadership* (London: Longmans)

ALLEN, V. L., 1966, *Militant Trade Unionism* (London: Merlin)

ALLEN, V. L., 1971, *The Sociology of Industrial Relations* (London: Longmans)

ANDERSON, P., 1965, 'Origins of the present crisis', in *idem* and Blackburn, R. (eds.), *Towards Socialism* (London: Collins)

ATHERTON, W. N., 1973, *A Theory of Union Bargaining Goals* (Princeton, at the University Press)

BAIN, G. S., 1970, *The Growth of White Collar Unionism* (Oxford, at the University Press)

BAIN, G. S., COATES, D. AND ELLIS, V., 1973, *Social Stratification and Unionism* (London: Heinemann)

BAIN, G. S. AND ELSHEIKH, F., 1976, *Union Growth and the Business Cycle* (Oxford: Blackwell)

BAIN, G. S. AND PRICE, R., 1976, 'Union growth revisited: 1948–74 in perspective', *Brit. Jnl of Ind. Rels.*, XIV, 3

BARITZ, L., 1960, *The Servants of Power* (Middletown: Wesleyan University Press)

BARRY, B., 1970, *Sociologists, Economists and Democracy* (London: Collier-Macmillan)

BATSTONE, E., BORASTON, I. AND FRANKEL, S., 1977, *Shop Stewards in Action* (Oxford: Blackwell)

BATSTONE, E., BORASTON, I. AND FRANKEL, S., 1978, *The Social Organization of Strikes* (Oxford: Blackwell)

BAUDOUIN, T., COLLIN, M. AND GUILLERM, D., 1978, 'Women and immigrants: marginal workers?', in Crouch, C. J. and Pizzorno, A. (eds.), Volume 2, *q.v.*

BERGER, S. (ed.), 1981, *Organizing Interests in Western Europe* (Cambridge, at the University Press)

BERGMANN, J., JACOBI, O. AND MÜLLER-JENTSCH, W., 1975,

Gewerkschaften in der Bundesrepublik (Frankfurt am Main: Europa Verlagsanstalt)

BEYME, C. VON, 1977, *Challenge to Power: Trade Unions and Industrial Relations in Capitalist Countries* (English edition, 1980, London: Sage)

BEYNON, H., 1973, *Working for Ford* (Harmondsworth: Penguin)

BLACKBURN, R., 1965, 'The new capitalism', in Anderson, P. and *idem* (eds.), *Towards Socialism* (London: Collins)

BLACKBURN, R., 1967, 'The unequal society', in *idem* and Cockburn, A. (eds.), *The Incompatibles: Trade Union Militancy and the Consensus* (Harmondsworth: Penguin)

BLACKBURN, R. M. AND MANN, M., 1979, *The Working Class in the Labour Market* (London: Macmillan)

BLAU, P., 1964, *Exchange and Power in Social Life* (New York: Wiley)

BOULDING, K. E., 1963, *Conflict and Defense* (New York: Harper and Row)

BRAVERMAN, H., 1974, *Labor and Monopoly Capital* (New York: Monthly Review Press)

BULLOCK, LORD, 1977, *Report of Committee of Inquiry into Industrial Democracy* (London: HMSO)

BURKITT, B., 1975, *Trade Unions and Wages* (Bradford, at the University Press)

CASTLES, S. AND KOSSACK, G., 1973, *Immigrant Workers and Class Structure in Western Europe* (London: Oxford University Press)

CHILD, J., LOVERIDGE, R. AND WARNER, M., 1973, 'Towards an organizational study of trade unions', *Sociology*, 7, 1

CLARKE, T., 1977, 'The *raison d'être* of trade unionism', in *idem* and Clements, L. (eds.), *q.v.*

CLARKE, T. AND CLEMENTS, L. (eds.), 1977, *Trade Unions under Capitalism* (London: Fontana)

CLAYRE, A. (ed.), 1980, *The Political Economy of Co-operation and Participation* (Oxford, at the University Press)

CLEGG, H. A., 1975: 'Pluralism in industrial relations', *Brit. Jnl of Ind. Rels.*, XIII, 3

CLEGG, H. A., 1976, *Trade Unionism under Collective Bargaining* (Oxford: Blackwell)

CLEGG, H. A., 1979, *The Changing System of Industrial Relations in Great Britain* (Oxford: Blackwell)

CLIFF, T., 1966, *Productivity Deals and How to Fight Them* (London: Pluto Press)

COLE, W. J., 1975, 'Research note: the financing of the individual striker: a case study in the building industry', *Brit. Jnl of Ind. Rels.*, XIII, 1

CREWE, I., 1982, 'The electoral decline of the Labour Party', in Kavanagh, D. (ed.), *The Politics of the Labour Party* (London: Allen and Unwin)

CROUCH, C. J., 1977, *Class Conflict and the Industrial Relations Crisis* (London: Heinemann)

CROUCH, C. J., 1979, *The Politics of Industrial Relations* (London: Fontana)

CROUCH, C. J., 1980, 'Varieties of trade union weakness: organized labour and capital formation in Britain, Federal Germany and Sweden', *West European Politics*, 3, 1

CROUCH, C. J., 1982, 'The peculiar relationship: the party and the unions', in Kavanagh, D. (ed.), *The Politics of the Labour Party* (London: Allen and Unwin)

CROUCH, C. J., forthcoming, 'The conditions of trade-union wage restraint', in Lindberg, L. N. and Maier, C. S. (eds.), *The Politics and Sociology of Global Inflation* (Washington, DC: Brookings Institution)

CROUCH, C. J. AND PIZZORNO, A. (eds.), 1978, *The Resurgence of Class Conflict in Western Europe since 1968*; Volume 1, *National Reports*; Volume 2, *Comparative Studies* (London: Macmillan)

CROZIER, M., 1964, *The Bureaucratic Phenomenon* (English edition, London: Tavistock)

DAHRENDORF, R., 1957, *Class and Class Conflict in Industrial Society* (English edition, 1959, London: Routledge and Kegan Paul)

DAHRENDORF, R., 1965, *Society and Democracy in Germany* (English edition, 1967, London: Weidenfeld and Nicolson)

Department of Employment Gazette, 1981, 'Developments in employee involvement', February–June, September

DUBOIS, P., DURAND, C. AND ERBÈS-SEGUIN, S., 1978, 'The contradictions of French trade unionism', in Crouch, C. J. and Pizzorno, A. (eds.), Volume 1, *q.v.*

DUNLOP, J. T., 1944, *Wage Determination and Trade Unions* (New York: Macmillan)

DUNLOP, J. T., 1958, *Industrial Relations Systems* (New York: Holt)

DURCAN, J. AND MCCARTHY, W. E. J., 1974, 'The state subsidy theory of strikes: an examination of statistical data for the period 1956–1970', *Brit. Jnl of Ind. Rels.*, XII, 1

EDELSTEIN, J. D. AND WARNER, M., 1975, *Comparative Union Democracy: Organization and Opposition in British and American Unions* (London: Allen and Unwin)

EDWARDS, R., 1979, *Contested Terrain* (London: Heinemann)

ELDRIDGE, J. E. T., 1968, *Industrial Disputes* (London: Routledge and Kegan Paul)

ELDRIDGE, J. E. T., 1971, *A Sociology of Industrial Life* (London: Nelson)

ELDRIDGE, J. E. T. AND CAMERON, G. C., 1964, 'Unofficial strikes: some objections considered', *Brit. Jnl of Sociol.*, XV, 1

ELVANDER, N., 1979, 'Sweden', in Roberts, B. C. (ed.), *Towards Industrial Democracy* (London: Croom Helm)

FLANDERS, A., 1964, *The Fawley Productivity Agreements* (London: Faber and Faber)

FLANDERS, A., 1965, *Industrial Relations: What is Wrong with the System* (London: Faber and Faber and Institute of Personnel Management)

FLANDERS, A., 1967, *Collective Bargaining: Prescription for Change* (London: Faber and Faber; first submitted as evidence to the Donovan Commission, 1966)

FLANDERS, A., 1970, *Management and Unions* (London: Faber and Faber)

FLANDERS, A. AND CLEGG, H. A., 1954, *The System of Industrial Relations in Great Britain* (Oxford: Blackwell)

FLANDERS, A. AND FOX, A., 1969, 'The reform of collective bargaining: from Donovan to Durkheim', *Brit. Jnl of Ind. Rels.*, VII, 2

FOX, A., 1966, *Industrial Sociology and Industrial Relations*, Research Paper No. 3 for Donovan Commission (London: HMSO)

FOX, A., 1973, 'Industrial relations: a critique of pluralist ideology', in Child, J. (ed.), *Man and Organization* (London: Allen and Unwin)

FOX, A., 1974a, *Beyond Contract: Work, Power and Trust Relations* (London: Faber and Faber)

FOX, A., 1974b, *Man Mismanagement* (London: Hutchinson)

FOX, A., 1979, 'A note on industrial relations pluralism', *Sociology*, 13, 1

FRÖBEL, F., HEINRICHS, J. AND KREYE, O., 1977, *The Changing International Division of Labour* (English edition, 1979, New York: Cambridge University Press)

FROW, R. AND E., AND KATANKA, M., 1971, *Strikes: a Documentary History* (London: Ch. Knight)

GALLIE, D., 1978, *In Search of the New Working Class* (Cambridge, at the University Press)

GENNARD, J., 1977, *Financing Strikes* (London: Macmillan)

GENNARD, J., DUNN, S. AND WRIGHT, M., 1980, 'The extent of closed shop arrangements in British industry', *Department of Employment Gazette*, January

GENNARD, J. AND LASKO, R., 1975, 'The individual and the strike', *Brit. Jnl of Ind. Rels.*, XIII, 3

GIDDENS, A., 1973, *The Class Structure of the Advanced Societies* (London: Hutchinson)

GLYN, A. AND SUTCLIFFE, B., 1972, *British Capitalism, Workers and the Profits Squeeze* (Harmondsworth: Penguin)

GOLDTHORPE, J. H., 1966, 'Attitudes and behaviour of car assembly workers', *Brit. Jnl of Sociol.*, September

GOLDTHORPE, J. H., 1974, 'Industrial relations in Great Britain: a critique of reformism', *Politics and Society* (reprinted in Clarke, T. and Clements, L. (eds.), 1977, *q.v.*, pp. 184–224, to which page numbers quoted here refer)

GOLDTHORPE, J. H., LOCKWOOD, D., BECHOFER, F. AND PLATT, J., 1968a, *The Affluent Worker: Industrial Attitudes and Behaviour* (Cambridge, at the University Press)

GOLDTHORPE, J. H., LOCKWOOD, D., BECHOFER, F. AND PLATT, J., 1968b, *The Affluent Worker: Political Attitudes and Behaviour* (Cambridge, at the University Press)

GOLDTHORPE, J. H., LOCKWOOD, D., BECHOFER, F. AND PLATT, J., 1969, *The Affluent Worker in the Class Structure* (Cambridge, at the University Press)

HARBISON, F. H., 1954, 'Collective bargaining and American capitalism', in Kornhauser, A., Dubin, R. and Ross, A. M. (eds.), *Industrial Conflict* (New York: McGraw Hill)

HEATH, A., 1976, *Rational Choice and Social Exchange* (Cambridge, at the University Press)

HEMINGWAY, J., 1978, *Conflict and Democracy: Studies in Trade Union Government* (Oxford: Clarendon Press)

HERDING, R., 1974, *Job Control and Union Structure* (Rotterdam, at the University Press)

HERZBERG, F., 1966, *Work and the Nature of Man* (Cleveland, Ohio: World Publishing Co.)

HERZBERG, F., 1967, *The Motivation to Work* (second edition, New York: Wiley)

HIBBS, D., 1978, 'On the political economy of long-run trends in strike activity', *Brit. Jnl of Pol. Sci.*, 8

HILL, S., 1981, *Competition and Control at Work* (London: Heinemann)

HINTON, J., 1973, *The First Shop Stewards' Movement* (London: Allen and Unwin)

HIRSCH, F. AND GOLDTHORPE, J. H. (eds.), 1978, *The Political Economy of Inflation* (Oxford: Martin Robertson)

HIRSCHMAN, A. O., 1970, *Exit, Voice and Loyalty* (Cambridge, Mass.: Harvard University Press)

HORTON, R., 1967, 'African traditional thought and Western science', *Africa*, XXXVII, 1 and 2

HUGHES, J., 1968, *Trade Union Structure and Government*, Research Paper No. 5 for Donovan Commission (London: HMSO)

HYMAN, R., 1971, *Marxism and the Sociology of Trade Unionism* (London: Pluto Press)

HYMAN, R., 1972, *Strikes* (London: Fontana)

HYMAN, R., 1975, *Industrial Relations: a Marxist Introduction* (London: Macmillan)

HYMAN, R. AND BROUGH, I., 1975, *Social Values and Industrial Relations* (Oxford: Blackwell)

INGHAM, G. K., 1970, *Size of Industrial Organization and Worker Behaviour* (Cambridge, at the University Press)

INGHAM, G. K., 1974, *Strikes and Industrial Conflict: Britain and Scandinavia* (London: Macmillan)

JACKSON, M. P., 1977, *Industrial Relations: a Textbook* (London: Croom Helm)

JACKSON, P. AND SISSON, K., 1976, 'Employers' confederations in Sweden and the United Kingdom and the significance of industrial infrastructure', *Brit. Jnl of Ind. Rels.*, XIV

KERR, C. AND SIEGEL, A., 1954, 'The inter-industry propensity to strike', in Kornhauser, A., Dubin, R. and Ross, A. M. (eds.), *Industrial Conflict* (New York: McGraw Hill)

KEYNES, J. M., 1936, *The General Theory of Employment, Interest and Money* (London: Macmillan)

LANE, A. D., 1974, *The Union Makes Us Strong* (London: Arrow)

LEGENDRE, M., 1978, *Les attitudes et les comportements des employés de bureau parisiens* (Paris: CORDES, CNRS, CSO)

LERNER, S. W., 1961, *Breakaway Trade Unions and the Small Trade Union* (London: Allen and Unwin)

LERNER, S. W. AND BESCOBY, A., 1966, 'Shop steward combine committees in the British engineering industry', *Brit. Jnl of Ind. Rels.*, IV, 2

LESTER, R. A., 1958, *As Unions Mature* (Princeton, at the University Press)

LIJPHART, A., 1976, *The Politics of Consociational Democracies* (Berkeley: University of California Press)

LIPSET, S. M., TROW, M. A. AND COLEMAN, U. S., 1956, *Union Democracy* (Glencoe, Ill.: Free Press)

LOCKWOOD, D., 1956, 'Social integration and system integration', *Brit. Jnl of Sociol.*, 7

LOCKWOOD, D., 1959, *The Blackcoated Worker* (London: Allen and Unwin)

MCCARTHY, W. E. J., 1964, *The Closed Shop in Britain* (Oxford: Blackwell)

MCCARTHY, W. E. J. (ed.), 1972, *Trade Unions* (Harmondsworth: Penguin)

MACDONALD, D. F., 1976, *The State and the Unions* (second edition, London: Macmillan)

MALLET, S., 1969, *La Nouvelle Classe Ouvrière* (fourth edition, Paris: Seuil)

MANN, M., 1973, *Consciousness and Action in the Western Working Class* (London: Macmillan)

MARGERISON, C. J., 1969, 'What do we mean by industrial relations? A behavioural science approach', *Brit. Jnl of Ind. Rels.*, VII, 3

MARSHALL, A., 1899, *Economics of Industry* (third edition, London: Macmillan)

MARTIN, R., 1968, 'Union democracy: an explanatory framework', *Sociology*, 2

MARTIN, R., 1978, 'The effects of recent changes in industrial conflict on the internal politics of trade unions: Britain and Germany', in Crouch, C. J. and Pizzorno, A. (eds.), Volume 2, *q.v.*

MASLOW, A. H., 1970, *Motivation and Personality* (second edition, New York: Harper and Row)

MAYO, E., 1949, *The Social Problems of an Industrial Civilization* (third edition, London: Routledge and Kegan Paul)

MICHELS, R., 1915, *Political Parties: a Sociological Study of the Oligarchical Tendencies of Modern Democracy* (English edition, Glencoe, Ill.: Free Press)

MOMMSEN, W. J., 1981, 'The German revolution 1918–1920: political revolution and social protest movement', in Bessel, R. and Feuchtwanger, E. J. (eds.), *Social Change and Political Development in Weimar Germany* (London: Croom Helm)

MORAN, M., 1974, *The Union of Post-Office Workers: a Study in Political Sociology* (London: Macmillan)

MORAN, M., 1977, *The Politics of Industrial Relations* (London: Macmillan)

MOSCA, G., 1896, *The Ruling Class* (English edition, 1936, New York)

MÜLLER-JENTSCH, W. AND SPERLING, H.-J., 1978, 'Economic development, labour conflicts and the industrial relations system in West Germany', in Crouch, C. J. and Pizzorno, A. (eds.), Volume 1, *q.v.*

NEWBY, H., 1977, *The Deferential Worker: a Study of Farm Workers in East Anglia* (London: Allen Lane)

NICHOLS, T. AND ARMSTRONG, P., 1976, *Workers Divided* (London: Fontana)

NICHOLS, T. (ed.), 1980, *Capital and Labour: a Marxist Primer* (London: Fontana)

OFFE, C., 1970, *Industry and Inequality* (English edition, 1976, London: Arnold)

OFFE, C. AND WIESENTHAL, H., 1980, 'Two logics of collective action: theoretical notes on social class and organizational form', *Political Power and Social Theory*, 1

OLSON, M., 1965, *The Logic of Collective Action: Public Goods and the Theory of Groups* (Cambridge, Mass.: Harvard University Press)

OLSON, M., 1978, 'The political economy of comparative growth rates' (University of Maryland, mimeo.)

PANITCH, L., 1976, *Social Democracy and Industrial Militancy* (Cambridge, at the University Press)

PANITCH, L., 1981, 'Trade unions and the capitalist state', *New Left Review*, 125, January/February

PARETO, V., 1923, *The Mind and Society* (English edition, 1935, London: Cape)

PARKIN, F., 1974, 'Strategies of closure in class formation', in *idem* (ed.), *The Social Analysis of Class Structure* (London: Tavistock)

PARKIN, F., 1979, *Marxism and Class Theory: a Bourgeois Critique* (London: Tavistock)

PATERSON, W. E. AND THOMAS, A. H. (eds.), 1977, *Social Democratic Parties in Western Europe* (London: Croom Helm)

PELLING, H. M., 1976, *A History of British Trade Unionism* (third edition, London: Macmillan)

PERLMAN, S., 1928: *A Theory of the Labor Movement* (New York: Macmillan)

PHELPS BROWN, E. H. WITH BROWNE, M., 1964, *A Century of Pay* (London: Macmillan)

PIZZORNO, A., 1978, 'Political exchange and collective identity in industrial conflict', in Crouch, C. J. and *idem* (eds.), Volume 2, *q.v.*

POOLE, M., 1981, *Theories of Trade Unionism: a Sociology of Industrial Relations* (London: Routledge and Kegan Paul)

PRIBIĆEVIĆ, S., 1959, *The Shop Stewards Movement and Workers' Control, 1910–22* (Oxford: Blackwell)

REGALIA, I., REGINI, M. AND REYNERI, E., 1978, 'Labour conflicts and industrial relations in Italy', in Crouch, C. J. and Pizzorno, A. (eds.), Volume 1, *q.v.*

REX, J., 1961, *Key Problems in Sociological Theory* (London: Routledge and Kegan Paul)

REYNAUD, J.-D., 1975, 'Trade unions and political parties in France: some recent trends', *Industrial and Labor Relations Review*, 28, 2

RICHTER, I., 1973, *Political Purpose in Trade Unions* (London: Allen and Unwin)

ROBERTS, B. C. (ed.), 1968, *Industrial Relations: Contemporary Problems and Perspectives* (second edition, London: Methuen)

ROBERTS, B. C., 1971, *Trade Unions: the Challenge before Them* (London: Industrial Education and Research Foundation)

ROBERTS, B. C., LOVERIDGE, R. AND GENNARD, J., 1972, *Reluctant Militants* (London: Heinemann)

ROBINSON, D., 1974, *Solidaristic Wage Policy in Sweden* (Paris: OECD)

ROETHLISBERGER, F. J. *et al.*, 1939, *Management and the Worker: an Account of a Research Project Conducted by the Western Electric Company, Hawthorne Works, Chicago* (Cambridge, Mass.: Harvard University Press)

ROGALY, J., 1977, *Grunwick* (Harmondsworth: Penguin)

ROSS, A. M., 1948, *Trade Union Wage Policy* (Berkeley: University of California Press)

ROSS, A. M. AND HARTMANN, P., 1960, *Changing Patterns of Industrial Conflict* (New York: Wiley)

ROY, D. F., 1980, 'Fear stuff, sweet stuff and evil stuff: management's defences against unionization in the South', in Nichols, T. (ed.), *q.v.*

ROYAL COMMISSION ON TRADE UNIONS AND EMPLOYERS' ASSOCIATIONS (DONOVAN COMMISSION), 1965a, *Minutes of Evidence No. 6: the Confederation of British Industry* (London: HMSO)

ROYAL COMMISSION ON TRADE UNIONS AND EMPLOYERS' ASSOCIATIONS (DONOVAN COMMISSION), 1965b, *Minutes of Evidence No. 12: Mr Cyril Grunfeld* (London: HMSO)

ROYAL COMMISSION ON TRADE UNIONS AND EMPLOYERS' ASSOCIATIONS (DONOVAN COMMISSION), 1966a, *Minutes of Evidence No. 16: National Federation of Building Trades Employers* (London: HMSO)

ROYAL COMMISSION ON TRADE UNIONS AND EMPLOYERS' ASSOCIATIONS (DONOVAN COMMISSION), 1966b, *Minutes of Evidence No. 20: Engineering Employers Association* (London: HMSO)

ROYAL COMMISSION ON TRADE UNIONS AND EMPLOYERS' ASSOCIATIONS (DONOVAN COMMISSION), 1966c, *Minutes of Evidence No. 23: Motor Industry Employers* (London: HMSO)

ROYAL COMMISSION ON TRADE UNIONS AND EMPLOYERS' ASSOCIATIONS (DONOVAN COMMISSION), 1966d, *Minutes of Evidence No. 31: Professor K. W. Wedderburn* (London: HMSO)

ROYAL COMMISSION ON TRADE UNIONS AND EMPLOYERS' ASSOCIATIONS (DONOVAN COMMISSION), 1966e, *Minutes of Evidence No. 44: Professor D. J. Robertson* (London: HMSO)

ROYAL COMMISSION ON TRADE UNIONS AND EMPLOYERS' ASSOCIATIONS (DONOVAN COMMISSION), 1966f, *Minutes of Evidence No. 62: Mr Allen Flanders* (see also under Flanders, A., 1967) (London: HMSO)

ROYAL COMMISSION ON TRADE UNIONS AND EMPLOYERS' ASSOCIATIONS (DONOVAN COMMISSION), 1968a, *Report*, Cmnd 3623 (London: HMSO)

ROYAL COMMISSION ON TRADE UNIONS AND EMPLOYERS' ASSOCIATIONS (DONOVAN COMMISSION), 1968b, *Selected Written Evidence* (London: HMSO)

RUNCIMAN, W. G., 1966, *Relative Deprivation and Social Justice* (London: Routledge and Kegan Paul)

SANI, G., 1979, 'Amici-nemici: parenti-serpenti: Communists and Socialists in Italy', in Brown, B. (ed.), *Eurocommunism and Eurosocialism* (New York: Cyrco Press)

SCHMITTER, P., 1979, 'Still the century of corporatism?', in *idem* and Lehmbruch, G. (eds.), *q.v.*

SCHMITTER, P. AND LEHMBRUCH, G. (eds.), 1979, *Trends towards Corporatist Intermediation* (Beverly Hills: Sage)

SHONFIELD, A., 1965, *Modern Capitalism* (Oxford, at the University Press)

SHORTER, E. AND TILLY, C., 1974, *Strikes in France: 1830–1968* (Cambridge, at the University Press)

SOREL, G., 1921, *Reflections on Violence* (English edition, 1925, London)

STEPHENS, J., 1979, *The Transition from Capitalism to Socialism* (London: Macmillan)

STEWART, A., PRANDY, K. AND BLACKBURN, R. M., 1980, *Social Stratification and Occupations* (London: Macmillan)

STREECK, W., 1980, 'Gewerkschaftsorganisation und industrielle Beziehungen: einige Stabilitätsprobleme industrieller gewerkschaftlicher Interessenverhaltung und ihre Lösung im westdeutschen System der industrielle Beziehungen', in Matthes, J. (ed.), *Sozialer Wandel in Westeuropa* (Frankfurt am Main: Campus)

SYLOS-LABINI, P., 1976, 'Competition: the product markets', in Wilson, T. and Skinner, A. S. (eds.), *The Market and the State* (Oxford: Clarendon Press)

TERRY, M., 1977, 'The inevitable growth of informality', *Brit. Jnl of Ind. Rels.*, XV, 1

THOMPSON, E. P., 1965, 'The peculiarities of the English', in Miliband, R. and Saville, J. (eds.), *The Socialist Register 1965* (London: Merlin)

THOMPSON, E. P., 1968, *The Making of the English Working Class* (second edition, Harmondsworth: Penguin)

TURNER, H. A., 1962, *Trade Union Growth, Structure and Policy: a Comparative Study of the Cotton Unions* (London: Allen and Unwin)

TURNER, H. A., CLACK, C. AND ROBERTS, G., 1967, *Labour Relations in the Motor Industry* (London: Allen and Unwin)

WAINWRIGHT, H., 1978, 'Women and the division of labour', in Abrams, P. (ed.), *Work, Urbanism and Inequality: UK Society Today* (London: Weidenfeld and Nicolson)

WEBB, B. AND S., 1897, *Industrial Democracy* (London: Longmans)

WEBB, B. AND S., 1920, *A History of Trade Unions* (second edition, London: Longmans)

WEBER, M., 1920, *Economy and Society* (English edition, 1968, New York: Bedminster Press)

WESTERGAARD, J. AND RESLER, H., 1975, *Class in a Capitalist Society* (London: Heinemann)

WILKINSON, F. AND TURNER, H. A., 1972, 'The wage-tax spiral and labour militancy', in Jackson, D. *et al.*, *Do Trade Unions Cause Inflation?* (Cambridge, at the University Press)

WOOD, S. AND ELLIOTT, R., 1977, 'A critical evaluation of Fox's radicalization of industrial relations theory', *Sociology*, 11, 1

Index of Names

Index of Subjects

Frank Field

INEQUALITY IN BRITAIN: FREEDOM, WELFARE AND THE STATE

This important book is a comprehensive review of poverty in Britain today, a new analysis of how living standards are determined by each of the five welfare states, and a political manifesto for the total reform of Britain's welfare system. Central to its argument is the idea that individual freedom is the true aim of socialism; greater equality the *means* to this end.

Frank Field, Labour MP for Birkenhead, puts poverty back into the centre of the political stage by arguing that in a no-growth economy reform must be paid for by redistribution of resources. And redistribution requires a complete reassessment not only of the traditional welfare state but also of the four other welfare states, which Frank Field now identifies as those provided by tax benefits, by companies, by private markets and by unearned incomes; these have increased inequalities in living standards over the last thirty years.

By adopting his suggestions for a radical reform of Britain's welfare states, the Labour Party would be pledging to combat poverty and to strengthen the power of ordinary people against the state, restoring to socialism its ultimate concern with freedom, and offering a vision of a just society which a new coalition of voters could support.

Robert Roberts

A RAGGED SCHOOLING

Life was harsh indeed in the tightly packed streets of industrial Salford in the years before the First World War. As he showed in his much acclaimed *The Classic Slum*, Robert Roberts knew at first hand the poverty and degradation which drove working men to seek oblivion from a pint glass, and their wives to pawn the family's Sunday best to buy bread.

But in the shadow of the factory chimneys a child could – and did – lead a life of tremendous vitality and excitement: games in the street and by the canal, daring excursions to mysterious foreign parts a mile or two down the road, flickering fantasies at the 'By Joe' cinema, the first whispered instruction in the dark pleasures of the flesh.

In this intimate and perceptive autobiography, Robert Roberts reveals the full texture and character of city life seen through the eyes of a child in the early years of the century. It is a remarkable piece of living history.

'The autobiography of an exceptional man . . . a memoir of quite extraordinary richness' – Paul Bailey, *Observer*

'A marvellous piece of work . . . this vivid portrait of a vanished community . . . bubbles with comic vitality' – Benny Green, *Spectator*

'Moving and enthralling . . . filled with humour, hope and human warmth' – Michael Kennedy, *Daily Telegraph*

'One of the best and most sensitive of English working-class autobiographies' – W. L. Webb, *Guardian*

Stephen Spender

THE THIRTIES AND AFTER

Since the 1930s, Stephen Spender, together with Auden, MacNeice and Day Lewis, has been identified with that decade when his poetry was first published. This collection of articles, reviews, memoirs and journals reflects both his personal concerns and his political preoccupations over the past five decades. He has introduced each decade with new essays describing the literary and political life of the time, thus providing a double perspective on the era.

The main themes of the book have their roots in the thirties, the decade of the Spanish Civil War and pre-war crises, when writers could no longer be non-political. But personal commitment to one ideology brought with it an awareness of the dangers, particularly acute for a writer, of surrendering individual freedom of choice and expression. These themes reverberate throughout the book, which ends with remembrances of Eliot, Connolly, MacNeice and Auden.

Stephen Spender's retrospective views of the decades together with the pieces published at the time make this book both a moving personal record by one of our finest writers and a fascinating case-history of a thirties poet and the times he has lived through.

Fontana Paperbacks: Non-fiction

Fontana is a leading paperback publisher of non-fiction, both popular and academic. Below are some recent titles.

- [ ] AN AUTOBIOGRAPHY Peter Alliss £1·95
- [ ] BOB HOPE: PORTRAIT OF A SUPERSTAR Charles Thompson £1·75
- [ ] SUBJECT WOMEN Ann Oakley £2·75
- [ ] HOW TO GET RID OF THE BOMB Gavin Scott £1·95
- [ ] POLICEMAN'S PATCH Harry Cole £1·50
- [ ] A YEAR IN THE DRINK Martin Green £1·75
- [ ] SCOTLAND introduction by Lord Home £4·95
- [ ] THE NO-DIET BOOK Michael Spira £1·50
- [ ] SIR JAMES GOLDSMITH Geoffrey Wansell £1·95
- [ ] THE CINDERELLA COMPLEX Colette Dowling £1·75
- [ ] DIANA, THE PRINCESS OF WALES Hugh Montgomery-Massingberd £1·95
- [ ] SONIA ALLISON'S FOOD PROCESSOR COOKBOOK £1·95
- [ ] THE ENTERTAINING COOKBOOK Evelyn Rose £3·95
- [ ] WAR AND SOCIETY IN REVOLUTIONARY EUROPE 1770–1870 Geoffrey Best £2·95
- [ ] EUROPEAN EMPIRES FROM CONQUEST TO COLLAPSE 1815–1960 Victor Kiernan £2·95
- [ ] DARWIN Wilma George £1·75
- [ ] THIS IS WINDSURFING Reinhart Winkler £5·95
- [ ] CHAMPION'S STORY Bob Champion & Jonathan Powell £1·50

You can buy Fontana paperbacks at your local bookshop or newsagent. Or you can order them from Fontana Paperbacks, Cash Sales Department, Box 29, Douglas, Isle of Man. Please send a cheque, postal or money order (not currency) worth the purchase price plus 10p per book (or plus 12p per book if outside the UK).

NAME (Block letters) _____

ADDRESS _____

_____

_____

While every effort is made to keep prices low, it is sometimes necessary to increase prices at short notice. Fontana Paperbacks reserve the right to show new retail prices on covers which may differ from those previously advertised in the text or elsewhere.